Teacher's Book R

Ages 4 – 5

Penny Coltman

Pearson Education Limited
Edinburgh Gate, Harlow, Essex CM20 2JE, England

First published 1999

ISBN 0 582 41994 3

Printed in China

Series consultant: Penny Coltman

Designed by Ken Vail Graphic Design Ltd, Cambridge

Photography by Gareth Boden

The Publishers' policy is to use paper manufactured from
sustainable forests.

Contents

Introduction

Numeracy Big Board and whole class teaching

Numeracy Big Board has been designed to meet the needs of teachers addressing the National Numeracy Strategy and, in Scotland, the recommendations in Improving Mathematics 5–14. It is the ideal solution to the challenge of whole class teaching, incorporating both books and equipment.

During whole class activities the Big Board functions as a lively and stimulating focus. Opportunities should be planned for children to interact with the board. Repetitive handling and positioning of the numbers, shapes and pictures will not only be enjoyable, but will help to consolidate learning.

When introducing teaching points, the equipment, in conjunction with the activities described in the books, provides illustrations of number facts and properties. Developing familiarity with the resource will help children to feel confident as it is used to support new learning.

This book provides detailed suggestions about how to use Numeracy Big Board to teach the whole class. The book is organised by content area, so look at your planning each week and select in advance the activities you want to use to fit in with your work for the week.

Numeracy Big Board and other parts of the Maths lesson

Although Numeracy Big Board has been designed with the problem of whole class teaching firmly in mind, the equipment can be used in other parts of your Maths lessons as well.

Whole class mental maths activities can be carried out using the Board and equipment.

As children separate into groups for differentiated tasks, the Big Board can be moved around the room to provide the basis of an independent group activity, or to facilitate further teaching.

In plenary sessions, the Big Board provides a medium for the compilation of summative statements relating to the lesson. Its interactive aspects will also allow groups and individuals to present ideas and findings to the rest of the class.

Using the resources

The Big Board is provided with overlays which include the most commonly used templates and visual aids needed to teach numeracy. Other formats can be drawn, or recordings made, on the white magnetic surface or the overlays using a dry wipe (i.e. water-based, non-permanent) marker pen.

Important: Take care never to write on the Big Board or the overlays with permanent ink!

Although many useful activities can be carried out with the overlays and writing alone, they become a much more flexible and interactive tool when used in conjunction with the magnetic cards.

The cards are designed to be durable, but are best stored safely in a tray when not in use. Explain to the children that, like any other magnets, the cards should be handled carefully.

As well as a wide range of other resources, a selection of character cards are included: elephants, monkeys, children and object cards 1–20. These cards will provide contexts for counting or calculation and will also encourage children to develop the skills of imagery when working with number. The elephants are printed in four colours and three sizes, so that they additionally form a useful basis for sorting, logic and pattern-based activities.

The coloured squares and dots can be used as counters or markers. They can also be used as an infinite selection of imaginary items to provide contexts for numeracy problems. Enjoy some lateral thinking!

Using the books

The books provide a selection of activities which suggest how the Big Board can be used in teaching most aspects of Number. At the end of the book there is a section of ideas about how to extend your use of the equipment into the other areas of the Maths curriculum.

To help you plan your numeracy teaching, the books are divided into double-page spreads. Each spread contains activities designed to address a particular area of learning. They are intended to be used to support your existing scheme of work for Mathematics. Select activities as and when they are appropriate, in order to meet your particular needs.

The activities can be repeated and varied many times to practise and develop the learning objectives concerned.

Each activity has:

- a clearly defined learning objective

  These objectives are linked to specific targets in the development of numeracy.

- a list of resources needed

  Nearly all the resources listed will be part of the Big Board apparatus. The only exceptions are occasional pieces of standard classroom equipment, such as dice or a puppet.

- preparation advice

  Sometimes it is helpful to have some cards in position on the Big Board at the beginning of the lesson. In other activities a drawn format or picture is required on the board.

- a description of the activity

  Familiarise yourself with this information before teaching the activity, in order to preserve spontaneity in your teaching.

  The information in this section includes:
  – a step-by-step guide to teaching the activity
  – opportunities to introduce interactive elements to the lesson
  – suggestions for productive questions.

In addition, many activities contain suggestions for extension.

Where appropriate, ideas are suggested for ways in which the Big Board apparatus can be further used to extend or challenge more able children.

Be creative!

This Teacher's Book will give you an invaluable starting point by providing a wealth of planned activities using Big Board. However, the list of activities described is only a beginning.

Big Board is intended to be enjoyable to use. As you become familiar with the equipment, explore its possibilities and enjoy supplementing the suggested activities with many more of your own ideas.

Links to the Framework for teaching mathematics

Unit 1: Beginning counting

- Recite the number names in order, continuing the count forwards or backwards from a given number.
- Count reliably up to 10 everyday objects (first to 5, then 10, then beyond), giving just one number name to each object. Recognise small numbers without counting.

Unit 2: More counting

- Say and use the number names in order in familiar contexts such as number rhymes, songs, stories, counting games and activities (first to 5, then 10, then 20 and beyond).
- Count reliably up to 10 everyday objects (first to 5, then 10, then beyond), giving just one number name to each object. Recognise small numbers without counting.

Unit 3: Numerals

- Count reliably up to 10 everyday objects (first to 5, then 10, then beyond), giving just one number name to each object. Recognise small numbers without counting.
- Begin to recognise 'none' and 'zero' in stories, rhymes and when counting.
- Count reliably in other contexts, such as clapping sounds or hopping movements.
- Recognise numerals 1 to 9, then 0 and 10, then beyond 10.

Unit 4: The number line to 10

- Recite the number names in order, continuing the count forwards or backwards from a given number.
- Count reliably up to 10 everyday objects (first to 5, then 10, then beyond), giving just one number name to each object. Recognise small numbers without counting.
- Begin to recognise 'none' and 'zero' in stories, rhymes and when counting.
- Recognise numerals 1 to 9, then 0 and 10, then beyond 10.

Unit 5: Counting to 20

- Say and use the number names in order in familiar contexts such as number rhymes, songs, stories, counting games and activities (first to 5, then 10, then 20 and beyond).
- Recite the number names in order, continuing the count forwards or backwards from a given number.
- Count reliably up to 10 everyday objects (first to 5, then 10, then beyond), giving just one number name to each object. Recognise small numbers without counting.
- Count reliably in other contexts, such as clapping sounds or hopping movements.
- Recognise numerals 1 to 9, then 0 and 10, then beyond 10.

Unit 6: Meeting larger numbers

- Count reliably up to 10 everyday objects (first to 5, then 10, then beyond), giving just one number name to each object. Recognise small numbers without counting.
- Recognise numerals 1 to 9, then 0 and 10, then beyond 10.

Unit 7: Counting in tens and twos

- Count reliably up to 10 everyday objects (first to 5, then 10, then beyond), giving just one number name to each object. Recognise small numbers without counting.
- Count reliably in other contexts, such as clapping sounds or hopping movements.
- Count in tens.
- Count in twos.
- Recognise numerals 1 to 9, then 0 and 10, then beyond 10.

Unit 8: Estimating

- Count reliably up to 10 everyday objects (first to 5, then 10, then beyond), giving just one number name to each object. Recognise small numbers without counting.
- Begin to recognise 'none' and 'zero' in stories, rhymes and when counting.
- Estimate a number in the range that can be counted reliably, then check by counting.
- Recognise numerals 1 to 9, then 0 and 10, then beyond 10.
- Use language such as more or less, greater or smaller, to compare two numbers and say which is more or less, and say a number which lies between two given numbers.

Unit 9: Comparing and ordering

- Count reliably up to 10 everyday objects (first to 5, then 10, then beyond), giving just one number name to each object. Recognise small numbers without counting.
- Begin to recognise 'none' and 'zero' in stories, rhymes and when counting.
- Recognise numerals 1 to 9, then 0 and 10, then beyond 10.
- Use language such as more or less, greater or smaller, to compare two numbers and say which is more or less, and say a number which lies between two given numbers.
- Order a given set of numbers: for example, the set of numbers 1 to 6 given in random order.
- Order a given set of selected numbers: for example, the set 2, 5, 1, 8, 4.
- Find one more or one less than a number from 1 to 10.

Unit 10: Number line puzzles

- Say and use the number names in order in familiar contexts such as number rhymes, songs, stories, counting games and activities (first to 5, then 10, then 20 and beyond).
- Begin to recognise 'none' and 'zero' in stories, rhymes and when counting.
- Recognise numerals 1 to 9, then 0 and 10, then beyond 10.
- Order a given set of numbers: for example, the set of numbers 1 to 6 given in random order.
- Order a given set of selected numbers: for example, the set 2, 5, 1, 8, 4.

Unit 11: Ordinal numbers

- Recognise numerals 1 to 9, then 0 and 10, then beyond 10.
- Begin to understand and use ordinal numbers in different contexts.

Unit 12: Addition 1 – combining sets

▶ Count reliably up to 10 everyday objects (first to 5, then 10, then beyond), giving just one number name to each object. Recognise small numbers without counting.
▶ Recognise numerals 1 to 9, then 0 and 10, then beyond 10.
▶ Begin to use the vocabulary involved in adding and subtracting.
▶ Begin to relate addition to combining two groups of objects, counting all the objects; extend to three groups of objects.

Unit 13: Addition 2 – counting on

▶ Say and use the number names in order in familiar contexts such as number rhymes, songs, stories, counting games and activities (first to 5, then 10, then 20 and beyond).
▶ Begin to recognise 'none' and 'zero' in stories, rhymes and when counting.
▶ Recognise numerals 1 to 9, then 0 and 10, then beyond 10.
▶ Begin to use the vocabulary involved in adding and subtracting.
▶ Find one more or one less than a number from 1 to 10.
▶ Begin to relate addition to counting on.

Unit 14: Using addition

▶ Say and use the number names in order in familiar contexts such as number rhymes, songs, stories, counting games and activities (first to 5, then 10, then 20 and beyond).
▶ Count reliably up to 10 everyday objects (first to 5, then 10, then beyond), giving just one number name to each object. Recognise small numbers without counting.
▶ Begin to recognise 'none' and 'zero' in stories, rhymes and when counting.
▶ Recognise numerals 1 to 9, then 0 and 10, then beyond 10.
▶ Begin to use the vocabulary involved in adding and subtracting.
▶ Begin to relate addition to combining two groups of objects, counting all the objects; extend to three groups of objects.
▶ Begin to relate addition to counting on.
▶ Begin to relate to addition of doubles to counting on.
▶ Find a total by counting on when one group of objects is hidden.
▶ Select two groups of objects to make a given total.

Unit 15: Subtraction 1 – partitioning sets

▶ Recite the number names in order, continuing the count forwards or backwards from a given number.
▶ Count reliably up to 10 everyday objects (first to 5, then 10, then beyond), giving just one number name to each object. Recognise small numbers without counting.
▶ Begin to recognise 'none' and 'zero' in stories, rhymes and when counting.
▶ Recognise numerals 1 to 9, then 0 and 10, then beyond 10.
▶ Begin to use the vocabulary involved in adding and subtracting.
▶ Separate (partition) a given number of objects into two groups.

Unit 16: Subtraction 2 – counting back

▶ Recite the number names in order, continuing the count forwards or backwards from a given number.
▶ Count reliably up to 10 everyday objects (first to 5, then 10, then beyond), giving just one number name to each object. Recognise small numbers without counting.
▶ Begin to recognise 'none' and 'zero' in stories, rhymes and when counting.
▶ Recognise numerals 1 to 9 then 0 and 10, then beyond 10.
▶ Begin to use the vocabulary involved in adding and subtracting.
▶ Separate (partition) a given number of objects into two groups.

Unit 17: More calculation

▶ Recite the number names in order, continuing the count forwards or backwards from a given number.
▶ Count reliably up to 10 everyday objects (first to 5, then 10, then beyond), giving just one number name to each object. Recognise small numbers without counting.
▶ Begin to recognise 'none' and 'zero' in stories, rhymes and when counting.
▶ Recognise numerals 1 to 9, then 0 and 10, then beyond 10.
▶ Begin to use the vocabulary involved in adding and subtracting.
▶ Begin to relate subtraction to 'taking away' and counting how many are left.
▶ Remove a smaller number from a larger and find how many are left by counting back from the larger number.
▶ Begin to find out how many have been removed from a larger group of objects by counting up from a number.
▶ Work out by counting how many more are needed to make a larger number.

Unit 18: Halves and doubles

▶ Count reliably up to 10 everyday objects (first to 5, then 10, then beyond), giving just one number name to each object. Recognise small numbers without counting.
▶ Count in tens.
▶ Count in twos.
▶ Recognise numerals 1 to 9, then 0 and 10, then beyond 10.
▶ Begin to use the vocabulary involved in adding and subtracting.
▶ Begin to relate to addition of doubles to counting on.
▶ Separate (partition) a given number of objects into two groups.
▶ Select two groups of objects to make a given total.
▶ Remove a smaller number from a larger and find how many are left by counting back from the larger number.
▶ Begin to find out how many have been removed from a larger group of objects by counting up from a number.

Unit 1: Beginning counting

① Number names

Learning objective	To memorise the sequence of number names from 'one' to 'five'.
Resources	• 5 coloured squares • 5 elephant cards

▶ Introduce the activity by repetitively singing the number names 'one' to 'five' to replace the words in a slightly adjusted tune of 'Twinkle, twinkle little star'. Show children how to raise the fingers of one hand one at a time as they count, or add claps, nods, hand shakes, leg taps, etc. to reinforce the number words with body movements.

▶ Continue by singing other favourite number rhymes which involve the numbers one to five. If you use counting rhymes which count backwards, such as 'Five currant buns', or 'Five speckled frogs', count the number of buns / frogs remaining, in between verses, to reinforce the forward sequence of number names. Use the coloured squares to represent the objects in the song, adding or removing them as appropriate.

▶ As children say the following traditional rhyme, add the elephant cards one at a time so that they form a line on the board.

One elephant went out to play,
Along a spider's web one day.
    (Children 'draw' web in the air)
He thought it such enormous fun,
    (Open arms to illustrate 'enormous')
That he called for another elephant to come.
    (Beckoning movements)

Two elephants ...

▶ Between each verse, encourage the children to predict the number of elephants which will now be in the line.

② Puppet counting

Learning objective	To develop early counting skills. In this activity children will use number sequencing, one-to-one matching and the understanding that the last number counted is the number of objects in the set.
Resources	• 5 face cards • a glove puppet

▶ Introduce the glove puppet as your friend who loves to count. The children are going to take it in turns to give her counting jobs to do.

▶ Show the children the face cards. Explain that they can choose a number of faces for the puppet to count. Demonstrate the idea by placing three faces in a line on the board and asking the puppet to count them.

▶ Use the puppet to count the cards from left to right. As each card is counted, 'help' by moving the card across the board, separating it from those which have not been counted. Encourage the children to count along with the puppet to help her. After counting the cards in each line ask the children:

So how many are there? (3)

▶ This will reinforce the idea that the last number word said is the number of cards in the set.

③ The careless puppet

Learning objective	To develop awareness of the possible errors in counting.
Resources	• 5 elephant cards • a glove puppet

▶ Explain that today the 'counting puppet' wants to try counting on her own. She is still very young and she might make mistakes. The children will need to watch her very carefully!

▶ As you use the puppet to count sets of elephant cards make occasional deliberate mistakes: start to count half-way along the line, repeat a number as you count, miss out a number, count the same card twice or miss one out. Encourage the children to identify the errors made and tell you what the correct count should have been.

▶ Ask the puppet how many cards she has counted. As the puppet replies (whispering in your ear) ask the children to confirm her answer. Again, making occasional mistakes after an apparently correct count will check that children understand that the last number counted represents the number of objects in the set.

Puppet says there were three elephants – is she right? (Yes)

④ Today's number

Learning objective	To become familiar with the numbers of objects represented by the number names 'one' to 'five' (cardinality).
Resources	• 5 face cards • 5 elephant cards • 5 coloured squares

▶ Place three square cards on the board. Ask the children to count the cards. Point to each card, touching it as it is counted.

How many cards are there? (3)
Who can hold up three fingers?

▶ Now ask a child to make a line on the board with three faces in it, and invite another child to make a line with three elephant cards. Each time count the line of cards together to check that there is the same number each time.

▶ Issue challenges to individual children:

Can you find me three pencils?
Can you find me three farm animals?
What can you find three of?

Extension

▶ This activity should be repeated on several occasions, using different numbers of objects from one to five.

⑤ Picture counting

Learning objective	To gain experience of counting objects which cannot be touched or moved.
Resources	• picture cards 1–5

▶ Place the one giraffe card on the board. Ask the children how many objects there are. Talk about how the children were able to tell you the number just by looking at the card, without touching or moving it.

▶ Repeat the activity with the two lions card.

How many objects are there? (2)

▶ Check by counting together.

▶ Allow the children to predict how many objects will be on the next card

▶ Repeat using the remaining cards with three, four and five objects. Invite individuals to say how many objects are on each card.

Extension

▶ Can the children still count the objects when the cards come in a surprise order? How quickly can they count? 'Shuffle' the cards and repeat.

Unit 2: More counting

① All spaced out

Learning objective	To understand that the number of objects in a set is unchanged by their position.
Resources	• 5 elephant cards

▶ Arrange one of the sets of five elephant cards in a fairly close line on the board and count them together with the children. Check that the children agree with you that there are five elephants in the line. Now spread the cards out, extending the length of the line. Ask the children:

How many elephants are in the line now? (5)

Note: Avoid saying 'Are there more elephants now?' as there can be linguistic confusion, since the elephants are taking up more space.

▶ Count the elephants again with the children and invite individuals to check that there are indeed still five elephants.

▶ Take the elephants off the board but show that you still have the cards in your hand, then replace them on the board in a different design. Again ask the children to predict how many elephants are now on the board, and to count them together.

▶ Repeat, using a variety of closely packed and widespread arrangements.

② Find the pairs

Learning objective	To recognise that the same number of objects can be arranged in different ways.
Resources	• sets of mixed coloured squares
Preparation	2 sets of 2 coloured squares 2 sets of 3 coloured squares 2 sets of 4 coloured squares 2 sets of 5 coloured squares Place all the sets of squares on the board. Arrange the two sets in each 'pair' differently.

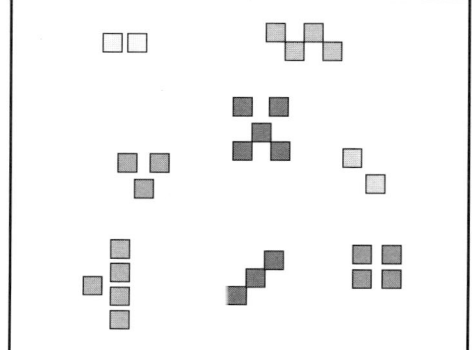

▶ Draw the children's attention to one of the sets of two squares.

Can anyone see the other set of two?

▶ Now invite one of the children to find a set of three.

Who can spot another set of three?

▶ Repeat until all the pairs of sets have been identified.

Extension

▶ Cover up one of the sets of squares. Can the children work out how many squares are in the covered set? (Encourage them to look for the set which is now left without a 'partner'.)

③ Starting points

Learning objective	To understand that the number of objects in a set is unchanged by the starting point of counting.
Resources	• 5 face cards

▶ Place the five face cards in a random, but not too widely spaced, arrangement on the board. Allow the children to choose a name for each face and write the name under each card.

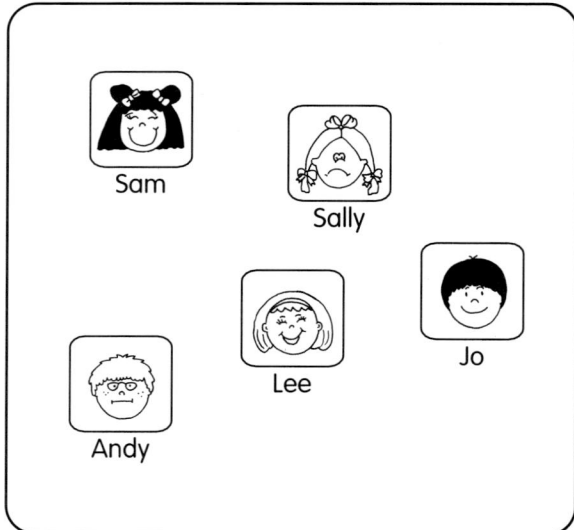

▶ Choose one child to come to the board and count the number of faces. Allow each face to be moved as it is counted if this helps the individual child, but return the faces to their original positions once the counting is finished.

▶ Draw attention to the face which was counted first.

▶ Pretend that you are able to hear the faces on the board having an argument. Each face wants to have a turn at being counted first. Invite a second child to help.

Can you count the faces but this time start with a different one?

▶ Repeat the activity until each face has been used as a starting point. Draw attention to the fact that the total remains unchanged.

Note: In carrying out this activity, avoid arranging the faces in a straight line. Being asked to start counting at the right-hand end of a line confuses children who have been taught to count from left to right. This is not such a problem if the faces are randomly arranged.

④ Give me five!

Learning objective	To develop the skill of counting out a given number of objects from a larger set and to reinforce the idea that the same number of cards can be differently arranged.
Resources	• 30–40 coloured squares

▶ Place the coloured squares at the bottom of the board. Invite a child to come to the board and to take five squares from the bottom of the board. Encourage counting aloud as each piece is removed. Now ask the child to place the five pieces in a pattern somewhere else on the board. Scribe the child's name beneath the pattern.

▶ Repeat with different children until all the square cards have been used. Look at the different patterns and arrangements which have been made. Talk about how each pattern still has five squares in it.

⑤ Number snap

Learning objective	To match sets of equivalent sizes.
Resources	• picture cards of objects 1–5 • 5 elephant cards • 5 face cards • coloured squares

▶ Place one of the picture cards on the board. Explain to the children that you do *not* want them to tell you how many objects are on the card. The idea of the game is that children decide how many objects are on the card and then place the same number of squares on the board. Offer the example that if there are two things on the card, they would put two coloured squares on the board. Talk about the importance of counting 'in their heads'.

▶ Choose a child to place an equivalent number of squares on the board, and encourage all the children to join in as the counting is checked.

▶ Repeat the activity using a different card, a line of faces or elephants as the initial counting challenge.

Unit 3: Numerals

① Introducing zero

Learning objective	To introduce numerals, including zero, as representations of number words.
Resources	• digit cards 0–5

▶ Place the digit card 5 at the right-hand side of the board. The children sing a favourite backward counting song, which begins with five objects, such as 'Five currant buns'. At the end of the first verse, as four buns are left, place the numeral 4 to the left of the 5.

▶ Continue to the end of the song. As the last bun is taken, and none are left, place the numeral 0 at the left-hand end of the line. Explain to the children that this is a way of representing nothing or none. It is usually called 'zero' or 'nought'.

▶ Read along the numbers from 0–5 with the children joining in the count.

Then enjoy the countdown as the children count backwards from 5–0, ending in a clap or a jump as the spaceship is launched!

② Is this your number?

Learning objective	To develop recognition of numerals.
Resources	• digit cards 0–5: one card per child • digit cards 0–5: 1 set

▶ Place a set of 0–5 digit cards on the board as a widely spaced number line. Distribute the remaining digit cards amongst the children.

▶ Read along the number line on the board with the children, pointing to each numeral in turn and saying its name. Now point to one of the numbers on the board.

Who is holding this number?
What is this number?

▶ Repeat for all the numerals along the 0–5 line.

▶ Once all the children are able to recognise the number they are holding, bring in some actions.

Stand up if you are holding a number 5.
Pat your head if you are holding a 0.
Stamp your feet if you are holding a number 4.

▶ And finally:

If you are holding a number 2 come and put your number under the number 2 on the board.

▶ Repeat for each numeral.

③ Action numbers

Learning objective	To develop recognition of numerals as a representation of quantity.
Resources	• digit cards 0–5

▶ Arrange the digit cards in order across the board. Read across the line with the children to reinforce number names.

▶ Explain that this time the children are going to clap the numbers as you point to them. So as you point to number 2 they are going to clap twice and so on.

What will happen when 0 is pointed to?

▶ Point to the numbers in sequence. As the children become confident in the game change the action to foot tapping, nodding, hand shaking, etc.

Extension

▶ Point to the numbers in random order.

How many times will 0 catch you out?

④ Spot the number

Learning objective	To develop recognition of numerals as a representation of quantity.
Resources	• digit cards 0–5 • 15 marker dots of assorted colours

▶ Arrange the marker dots in a group at the bottom of the board. Place the digit card 1 towards the left-hand side of the board. Now invite children to offer to find 'that number of spots' to put beneath the number.

▶ Repeat using the numerals 2 to 5 in sequence.

What should we do about 0?

▶ Encourage children to suggest that 0 should be placed at the left-hand end of the line but will have 0 spots beneath it.

Extension

▶ Remove the digit cards and replace the spots at the bottom of the board. Shuffle the digit cards and invite children in turn to pick a card, magician style, place it anywhere on the board, and invite others to find the correct numbers of spots to place next to it. Clear the board between turns.

⑤ Find the pairs

Learning objective	To develop recognition of numerals as a representation of quantity.
Resources	• picture cards 1–5 • number cards 1–5

▶ Scatter the picture cards and number cards in a random arrangement over the lower half of the board. Invite the children to spot the pairs of matching number and picture cards.

▶ As each pair is found ask the finder to say the number represented by the numeral and picture.

▶ Encourage the rest of the class to check the counting and the match, and then place the two cards together in the top half of the board.

⑥ Word spotting

Learning objective	To develop the recognition of number words.
Resources	• digit cards 0–5 • word cards from 'zero' to 'five' • picture cards from 1–5

▶ Place the digit cards in a widely spaced line, in sequence across the top of the board. Read the numerals with the children.

▶ Show the children the picture cards and invite volunteers to match each picture with its digit card, placing the pictures beneath the numerals.

Why is there no picture card for 0?

▶ Now introduce the word cards. Read each in turn and draw attention to initial sounds. Place each word beneath the corresponding numeral / picture pair.

▶ Finally, ask the children to read each digit card again, count the objects on the picture card and draw the related numeral in the air.

Unit 4: The number line to 10

In addition to the activities in this Unit, many of the activities in Units 1–3 can be easily adapted to familiarise children with the numbers 6–10.

① Number line towers

Learning objective	To consolidate numeral recognition to 10.
Resources	• number line overlay • coloured squares
Preparation	Place the number line across the middle of the board. As a large number of coloured squares will be needed for this activity it will be most convenient to have them in a box available for children to use.

▶ With the children, read the numbers across the number line.

▶ Return to the beginning of the line and explain to the children that they are going to use the coloured squares to build a tower on each number. Show the children how above the number 1 there is going to be a tower of just 1 square. Place the one square above the number 1.

What will be above the 0 card?

▶ Invite individual children to come to the board to build the number towers. As each tower is built from the coloured squares ask the rest of the children to count the squares used.

▶ Talk to the children about the towers made, drawing attention to the resulting 'staircase' shape. Ask questions:

Who can spot the tower made from seven bricks?
How many squares are in the tallest tower?

Extension

▶ Introduce word cards to match to the corresponding towers.

② Odd one out

Learning objective	To consolidate numeral recognition to 10.
Resources	• digit cards 0–10 • word cards 'zero' to 'ten' • picture cards 1–10 • puppet (as in Unit 1)

▶ Talk to the children about the different ways of showing numbers which they have met.

▶ Show as an example a set with the digit card, word card and the picture card all representing the same number, e.g. 6, 'six' and picture card for 6.

▶ Now explain to the children that the careless puppet is going to make some sets. They will need to watch carefully to spot her mistakes.

▶ Use the puppet to place another set of three cards on the board, but include one error, e.g. 4, 'four', but picture card for 5.

▶ Repeat several times, remembering to use 0. Occasionally allow the puppet to 'get it right' as a surprise!

③ Counting forwards, counting backwards

Learning objective	To further develop familiarity with the order of numbers to 10.
Resources	• 10 face cards • digit cards 0–10
Preparation	Place the face cards in a row across the middle of the board. Place the digit cards across the bottom of the board in random order.

▶ Start by asking the children to count the faces on the board.

Everyone hold up ten fingers.

▶ Then sing the song 'Ten in a bed'. At the end of each verse remove one face from the board and repeat questions similar to those above.

▶ At the end of the song explain that now you are going to put all the children back into bed. As each face is returned to the 'bed' ask volunteers to choose a number from the bottom of the board. The numbers are placed by the faces and will form a number line above them.

Where will the 0 go?

▶ Finish the activity by counting forwards to 10, and back to 0.

④ Number line quiz

Learning objective	To develop familiarity with the 0–10 number line.
Resources	• digit cards 0–10
Preparation	Place the numeral 0 at the right-hand side of the board. Distribute the remaining digit cards (1–10) to individual children.

▶ Start by building the number line. Point out the 0 card on the board.

What number comes after 0?
Who has that card?

▶ Each card is thus added to the number line in turn.

▶ Once the line is complete ask questions such as:

Who can point to a number next to 8?
Who can point to a number between 4 and 6?
Who can point to a number 3?

⑤ Take a ladybird for a walk

Learning objective	To introduce the concept of 'one count – one move'.
Resources	• number line overlay • red marker dot to represent a ladybird

▶ Explain to the children that today they have a visiting ladybird. Like all animals their ladybird needs exercise. They are going to take her for walks along their number line. The ladybird likes to count as she walks.

▶ Start with the ladybird on 0 and count along the number line as she is moved to 10. Emphasise the 'one count – one move' rule.

▶ Place the ladybird back at the beginning of the line and explain to the children that they are going to count the number of steps the ladybird takes. Move the ladybird along the line to number 5 counting 1, 2, 3, 4, 5 steps.

▶ Now suggest puzzles for the children to solve.

Ladybird wants to walk from 3 to 6. How many steps will she take? (3)
Ladybird wants to walk from 2 to 7. How many steps will she take? (5)

▶ Each time, as checking occurs, enforce the 'one count – one move' rule.

Note: At this stage the process is only about counting steps. There should be no suggestion of counting on or back as addition or subtraction.

Unit 5: Counting to 20

① Count to 20

Learning objective	To recite the numbers from 11–20.
Resources	• 20 coloured squares

▶ Place all twenty coloured squares, in two rows of ten, on the board. Count the first row of ten squares with the children.

But there are more squares – what shall we do now?

▶ Allow children to make suggestions. Then count on slowly encouraging the children to repeat the numbers after you.

▶ Read a number rhyme to twenty such as '1, 2, Buckle my shoe', pointing to the numbers as you go and encouraging the children to join in saying the number names.

Extension

▶ Invite children to remember some of the names of numbers up to 20. In each case count along the squares on the board, reinforcing the counting sequence:

Seventeen. That's a good number. Let's count the squares up to seventeen.

② A number story

Learning objective	To develop familiarity with the numbers from 11–20.
Resources	• number cards 11–20

▶ In this activity you are going to tell the children a story which contains the numbers 11–20. Each time a number is mentioned in the story, show the children the appropriate numeral and place it on the board, gradually building a number line. Each number is also clearly associated with actions to count, to further consolidate the sequence of number names.

*In a dark, dark cave, a long time ago, lived a dragon. He had been all alone for a thousand years and was very sad and lonely. One day he woke up from a long sleep and gently picked off the **eleven** spiders who had made their webs on his wings whilst he was asleep. Then he slowly stood up and did his dragon exercises. First he stamped his feet **twelve** times. Then he bent his knees **thirteen** times, and finally he flapped his wings **fourteen** times.*

The dragon wandered over to his treasure chest and opened the lid. Good. All his treasure was still there.

*Carefully, because they were very heavy, he counted out his **fifteen** gold bars.*

*Now the dragon was hungry. He found his huge dragon feeding bowl and poured **sixteen** jars of honey into it from his store cupboard.*

*Next he decided to see what was happening in the world and wandered over to the entrance of his cave. It was a bright sunny day, and the dragon blinked **seventeen** times. Just then he heard a noise. There was laughter and music. It was coming from the other side of the hill.*

*What could be going on? The dragon took **eighteen** heavy steps to reach the top of the hill.*

Just on the other side, the dragon found a birthday picnic in full swing. It was a royal party for the young prince's birthday. The prince walked over to the dragon.

'Could you help me?' he asked. 'We seem to have forgotten the royal matches to light the candles on my cake.'

*The dragon did as he was asked, using just a small roar of flame (because he didn't want to burn the cake), and then joined in as everyone helped to blow out the **nineteen** candles.*

*'Please be the royal dragon,' said the prince, 'and come to live in the palace with us.' And everyone clapped **twenty** times because they were so delighted.*

③ Pick a number

Learning objective	To count from a given starting point.
Resources	• number cards 1–20 • 20 elephant cards
Preparation	Place the number cards on the board in sequence, in four widely spaced rows of five, with an elephant card above each number.

► Explain to the children that they are going to practise counting to 20. Count along the elephant rows starting with number 1.

► Now tell the children that some of the other elephants would like a turn at being the first to be counted. Allow children to take turns in choosing a number between 1 and 20 to be the starting point for counting.

Note: In each case the counting is going to be along the line from left to right stopping at 20.

Extension

► Can the children count to 20 starting at any number with their eyes closed? Return to the board to consolidate.

④ Picture card count

Learning objective	To accurately count larger sets of objects.
Resources	• picture cards 10–20 • number cards 10–20

► Sort the picture cards into numerical order. Place the ten bananas picture card on the board and count the objects with the children. Choose a volunteer to find the correct number card to place on the board next to the picture.

Who can remember what number comes after 10?

► Continue until all the cards to 20 have been counted.

Extension

► Remind the children about previous counting experiences. Would choosing different starting points on the pictures make any difference to the number of objects counted?

⑤ Number spotting

Learning objective	To accurately count larger sets of objects.
Resources	• number cards 11–20 • marker dots of assorted colours
Preparation	Scatter the marker dots over the bottom of the board.

► Invite individuals to each choose one of the number cards. The card is placed on the board and the chooser, with help from the 'audience', counts out the equivalent number of marker dots to place by the number card.

► Then remove all number cards and marker dots from the board. Place a number (from 11 to 20) of marker dots on the board and challenge the children to count them. Talk about the different methods of counting.

Is it helpful to move the spots so that we know which have been counted?

► In some cases invite two children to count the same group of spots.

Do they reach the same number?
If their counts are different what might this tell us?

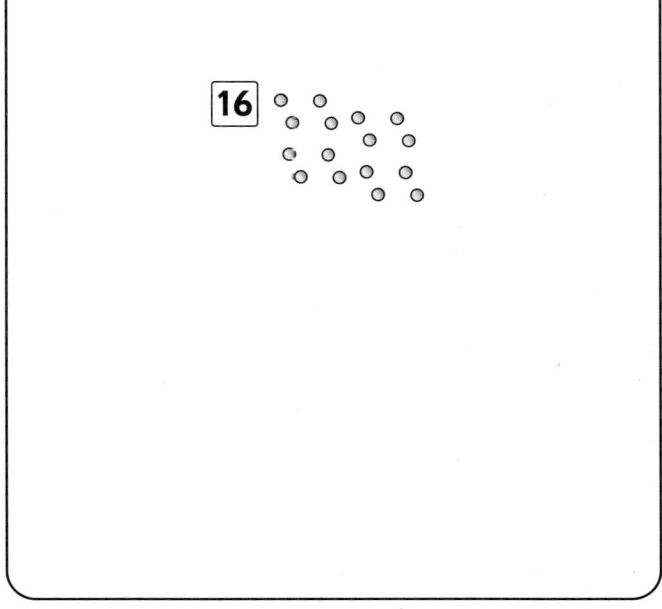

Unit 6: Meeting larger numbers

① Thinking big

Learning objective	To develop awareness of numbers beyond 20.
Resources	• number cards 1–100 • individual cards to allow for the making of numbers greater than 100 • marker pen

► Start by choosing a selection of six numbers between 21 and 49 and placing them on the board. Tell the children that these numbers are your choice of lottery numbers for this week.

Can anybody say what these numbers are?

► Read the numbers to the children and explain that these are all numbers larger than 20.

Can anybody think of any other numbers larger than 20?

► Some children may have birthdays towards the end of a month, others may live in houses with high numbers. Talk to the children about bus numbers, the number of children in the class or the year number.

What is meant by 'the millennium'?

► In each case record the numbers discussed on the board. Record number words which children use such as 'hundred', 'thousand' or 'million'.

Extension

What is the biggest number you can think of?

► Record ideas on the board.

Is that really the biggest number?
Could we ever stop counting?

② Counting to a hundred

Learning objective	To develop familiarity with the sequence of numbers to 100.
Resources	• 100 coloured squares
Preparation	Arrange the coloured squares in ten rows of ten (random colours).

► Explain to the children that they are going to help you to count all the coloured squares.

How many squares do you think there might be?

► As you count the squares together draw particular attention to the changes in vocabulary as the decades change. Enjoy the moment of reaching the grand total of a hundred!

► Go back to the counting and remind the children of the names of the different decades. Talk about how the change is signalled by a 9, i.e. 19, *twenty* ... 29, *thirty* ... 39, *forty* ..., etc.

Extension

► Place part of an additional row of squares on the board.

What would happen if there were more than a hundred squares?

③ Pirate cave adventure! (Keeping count)

Learning objective	To reliably count sets of objects using numbers beyond 20.
Resources	• 30–40 marker dots of assorted colours
Preparation	Randomly scatter the marker dots over the lower half of the board. Above them draw a large rectangle.

► With the board turned around, tell the children a story about a secret cave which they discovered whilst on a school outing. During their adventures in the cave they came across a pirates' treasure chest full of precious jewels! But – oh dear – they have dropped it on their way out of the cave.

► Turn the board around to reveal the scattered dots. Here are the jewels: emeralds, rubies, sapphires and diamonds!

► Ask for volunteers to help to count the jewels. Allow two or three children to count the jewels and talk about any discrepancies in their answers. Discuss how difficult it is to remember which jewels have been counted and which have not.

How could we solve this problem?

▶ Encourage the conclusion that it is helpful to move the jewels as they are counted. Draw attention to the rectangle at the top of the board. This is the treasure chest. The jewels are then counted as they are put away.

Extension

▶ One of the difficulties in remembering which jewels have been counted is that they are placed at random.

How might we put them in the box to help us remember the count? (Encourage the use of rows.)

④ Find the teddy

Learning objective	To develop recognition of numerals to 100.
Resources	• small paper cut-out of teddy shape • number cards 21–30 • Blu-tack

▶ Show the children the number cards 21–30. Place them in order on the board and read along the line of numbers with the children.

Who can point to 26?

What number is next to 21?

▶ Show the children the small cut-out teddy. Explain that the teddy is going to hide behind one of the numbers and they have to find him.

▶ Without the children seeing, place the teddy behind one of the numbers, holding him in place

with a small piece of Blu-tack. As children guess the number of the hiding place encourage them to both say and locate the number before removing it to see if their guess was right.

▶ The child who is lucky in finding the teddy has the next turn in hiding it for others to locate.

Extension

▶ As children become confident in identifying numbers to 30, extend to different decades of numbers, occasionally returning to lower numbers as reinforcement activities.

⑤ Hundred square counting

Learning objective	To introduce the 100 square.
Resources	• 100 square overlay • coloured squares
Preparation	Place one coloured square on each square of the hundred square, covering the numerals.

▶ Remind the children about the square counting activity. Explain that here is another large number of squares for them to count.

How many do you think there are?

▶ This time as each square is counted you are going to remove it from the board.

▶ Start counting and removing squares. Stop after five or six squares have been counted and removed.

What can you see behind the squares?

▶ As each square is removed from the units digit 9, pause and encourage some predictions.

What is the next number going to be?

What might it look like?

Unit 7: Counting in tens and twos

① Action tens

Learning objective	To consolidate the sequence of numbers when counting in tens to a hundred.
Resources	• number cards 10, 20, 30, 40, 50, 60, 70, 80, 90, 100 • 100 coloured squares
Preparation	Place the coloured squares in ten rows of ten.

▶ With the children count the coloured squares. At the end of each row of ten squares place the appropriate number card, denoting the total count 'so far'.

▶ Explain to the children that counting in tens can be a quick way of counting.

It is useful to be able to 'count in tens'.

▶ Read down the list of tens numbers with the children, encouraging them to join in as soon as they feel able.

▶ Now place actions with each number word. For example:

Ten	*(Place right hand on head)*
Twenty	*(Place left hand on head)*
Thirty	*(Place right hand on right shoulder)*
Forty	*(Place left hand on left shoulder)*
Fifty	*(Right hand taps right leg)*
Sixty	*(Left hand taps left leg)*
Seventy	*(Stamp right foot)*
Eighty	*(Stamp left foot)*
Ninety	*(Spin round on spot)*
A hundred	*(Clap hands above head)*

▶ Repeat frequently to reinforce the sequence of number words.

② Jumping tens

Learning objective	To consolidate the sequence of numbers when counting in tens to a hundred.
Resources	• number cards 0, 10, 20, 30, 40, 50, 60, 70, 80, 90, 100 • 1 green square
Preparation	Draw a zig-zag track of eleven lily pad shapes down the board. Place the number cards in sequence, one on each lily pad.

▶ Explain to the children that this is a special pond. The lily pads in the pond have all the 'counting in tens' numbers to a hundred. Read down the lily pad trail with the children joining in the counting in tens.

▶ Introduce the green square and explain that this is a green frog who lives in the pond. He likes to count in tens as he jumps between the lily pads. They can help him to count, but they must remember the rule: one count – one move.

▶ Starting on the 0, jump the frog down the trail with the children counting as he goes. Vary the speed of his jumps to ensure that the children are watching carefully, saying the words to match the jumps.

▶ Now suggest some puzzles:

If the frog starts on 0 and makes two jumps, where will he land? (20)

If the frog starts on 20 and makes three jumps where will he land? (50)

▶ Allow individuals to move the frog as the predictions are checked.

Note: All jumps are forward, and there is no suggestion of addition; this is merely a counting activity.

Extension

▶ Draw one more lily pad on the board.

What would be the number of the next lily pad in the trail?

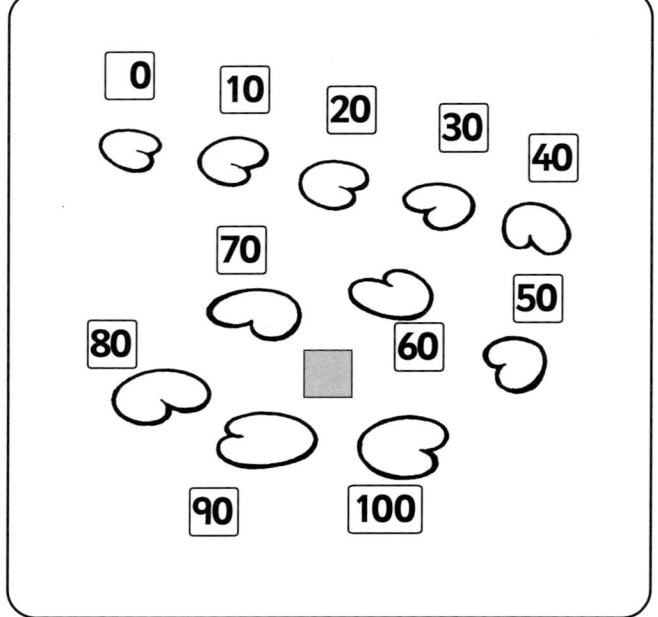

③ Animal twos

Learning objective	To introduce counting in twos.
Resources	• number cards 0, 2, 4, 6, 8, 10, 12, 14, 16, 18, 20 • marker dots of assorted colours

▶ Introduce the following rhyme, allowing children to choose the animal for each repetition and encouraging sound effects!

Noah had animals,
Just like the zoo.
He had tigers
    (roar, roar)
And he had <u>two</u>.
    (clap as word 'two' is said)

▶ After each verse place a pair of dots on the board to represent the two new additions to the ark, and ask:

How many animals now?

▶ Place the appropriate number card next to the pair to indicate the current running total. Explain to the children that they have been counting in twos, just like Noah must have done.

▶ Complete the activity by reading down the list of numerals in the animal parade.

④ Skip counting

Learning objective	To develop familiarity with the sequence of numbers when counting in twos.
Resources	• number cards 1–20
Preparation	Arrange the number cards in two rows of ten across the board.

▶ Explain to the children that they are going to learn to count in twos. They are going to count to twenty, tapping their legs and clapping like this:

one two three four five six seven eight nine ten
tap clap tap   clap tap clap tap   clap   tap clap

         and so on.

▶ As the children count, move your finger along the number line, raising the position of the 'clap' numbers. Draw the children's attention to these numbers.

▶ Now suggest to the children that they are only going to whisper the numbers when they tap their knees, but the clapping numbers are going to be said normally. The rule is 'whisper a number, say a number'.

▶ Once children are confident in this, change the rule to '*think* a number, say a number'. Now the children are only saying the raised, or clapping numbers.

▶ Over time, the claps and taps can be phased out, as children become fluent in counting in twos.

Extension

▶ Encourage children to add numbers, continuing the line on the board.

⑤ Elephants on the bus

Learning objective	To use the skill of counting in twos in a practical context.
Resources	• set of elephant cards
Preparation	Draw a line down the centre of the board. Then draw several horizontal lines across the board so that it is divided into paired sections. (Check that each section is at least 5 cm deep and 10 cm wide.)

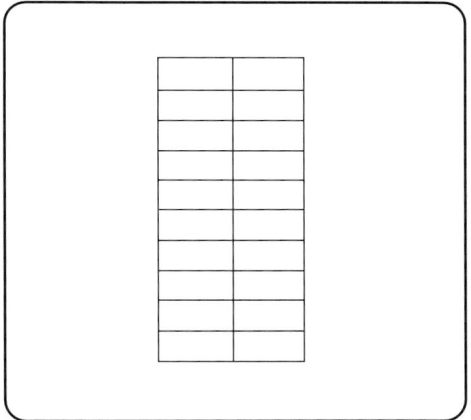

▶ Tell the children a story about an elephant school in the jungle. The elephant children are going on an outing.
Each box on the board is a seat on the jungle bus. Two elephants can sit on each seat.

▶ Encourage children to gradually add elephants to the bus, ensuring that 'complete' seats are filled at each addition. After each addition ask:

How many elephants are on the bus now?

▶ Encourage the children to count in twos to find out the answer.

Extension

▶ Use an additional elephant card to pose the problem:

What happens if there is only one elephant on one of the seats?

Unit 8: Estimating

① How many are there?

Learning objective	To develop estimation skills using small numbers of objects.
Resources	• picture cards 1–10

▶ Tell the children that you are going to see how good they are at estimating. Explain that estimating is a bit like guessing, but an estimate is a 'thought about guess'.

▶ Start by saying that you are going to place a picture card on the board, just for a few seconds – not long enough to count – and that they are going to estimate how many pictures were on the card.

▶ Place the three parrots picture card on the board for a few seconds and then remove it.

How many parrots were there? (3)

▶ Children should confidently say 'three'.

Do you mean 'about three', or 'exactly three'?

▶ Try again with another small number picture card, and then use a larger number card such as the nine crabs card to show that as the numbers increase it is less easy to be quite so certain in the estimates! Check the number by counting.

How close were you in your guess?

▶ Reinforce vocabulary such as 'about' and 'nearly' in making estimates. Words such as 'close', 'accurate' or 'surprising' can be useful in discussing the estimates or the checked result.

② Elephants line up

Learning objective	To develop estimation skills using hidden objects.
Resources	• 2 red squares • 20 elephant cards • marker pen
Preparation	Draw a straight horizontal line across the middle of the board.

▶ In this activity the children are going to estimate how many elephants will fit in a space.

▶ Place the two squares about a ruler length apart on the line.

▶ Explain to the children that the elephants are going to go on a journey. They need help in choosing a truck to travel on. The line on the board represents the back of one of the trucks. How many elephants do the children think would fit on this truck?

Remember that the elephants must be able to stand side by side.

▶ Collect estimations from the children, recording them at the bottom of the board. Then involve children in the counting as the elephant cards are placed in the space.

▶ Use the opportunity to introduce vocabulary: 'exactly', 'almost', 'not quite', 'nearly', 'not quite', 'enough', etc.

▶ Repeat, moving the red squares to represent different vehicles which the elephants try out.

Extension

▶ Reverse the problem:

Ten elephants want to be able to fit on the truck.
How long do you think the truck would need to be?
Use the squares to show me.

③ Too many, too few

Learning objective	To extend the vocabulary of estimation.
Resources	• face cards • 12 red marker dots • 7 blue marker dots • 11 yellow marker dots • 8 green marker dots • 10 red squares

▶ Tell the children that they are going to help with a birthday party. Place the ten faces on the board and explain that these are the guests. Count them with the children.

▶ The shopping has already been done for the party but have the right amounts been bought?

▶ Firstly each guest will need a balloon. Have we enough? Quickly place the twelve red marker dots on the board and ask the children to decide whether or not there will be enough. What do they think? Cover the spots with your hand after a few seconds to discourage counting!

▶ Check by counting.

Thank goodness – there are plenty!

▶ Continue with the game using the different coloured markers to represent different party requirements.

▶ Introduce and reinforce the vocabulary: 'about enough', 'too many', 'not enough', 'too few', 'exactly the right amount', 'nearly enough', etc.

④ What do you think?

Learning objective	To develop estimation skills within a practical context.
Resources	• digit cards 1–9, in sets • marker pen • thirty-second timer or clock with clear second hand • 12 elephant cards, all different
Preparation	Divide the board, using 'noughts and crosses' lines, into nine sections. Place a digit card in each section.

▶ In this activity children are going to estimate how many times an action can be repeated in half a minute.

▶ Divide the class into small groups of, preferably, two or three children. Each group is given one of the elephant cards. This card is their 'marker'.

▶ Before each activity is carried out, each group must discuss the challenge, decide on their estimate and place their marker in the appropriate 'box' on the board. Some activities might be for the whole group to perform and some might be for individuals.

Examples:

Balance blocks in a tower
Thread beads
Write name
Sing a nursery rhyme
Say or read the alphabet

Which groups were the good estimators?

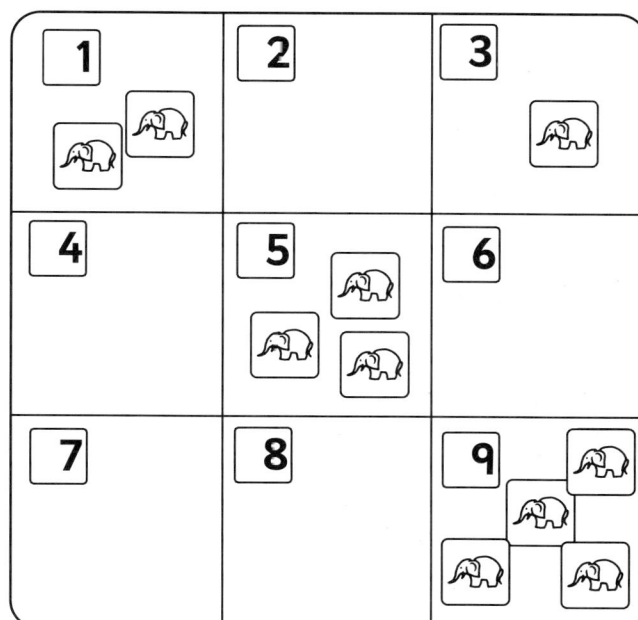

⑤ Estimating larger numbers

Learning objective	To develop estimation skills using larger numbers.
Resources	• picture cards 11–20 • marker dots of assorted colours • jar or box of beads

▶ In this activity children are going to practise making estimates of larger numbers.

▶ Start by using the picture cards, showing each for a few seconds before collecting estimates of number.

▶ Use the marker dots to provide numbers above twenty, scattering them randomly over the board.

▶ Finally show children the jar of beads. Perhaps they have played a game like this at a fund-raising event.

How many beads do you think are in the jar?

▶ This is more difficult because the beads cannot be individually seen.
Encourage 'more than', 'less than' and 'about' in describing number

Who thinks there are more than a hundred?
Less than fifty?
About thirty?

Extension

▶ Without overlapping, cover an area of the board with marker dots. Allow individuals to estimate how many dots they could cover with one hand. Remove surrounding dots whilst the hand is held on the board to then allow counting.

Unit 9: Comparing and ordering

① More than, less than and the same

Learning objective	To develop comparative language.
Resources	• 6 face cards • marker pen
Preparation	Draw two large circles on the board. Place the face cards at the top of the board.

▶ Explain to the children that the face cards represent some children coming to school. When the children get to school they can choose which activity they go to.

▶ The two circles represent two different activities. Invite the children to decide what those activities are. Draw a symbol in each circle to remind children of their choice.

▶ In turn work along the line of faces, allowing the children to decide which activity each 'child' will go to. When all the faces have been allocated to a circle, talk about the two sets of faces.

Note: This activity should not involve counting. The idea is to make visual comparisons between sets.

▶ Reinforce comparative vocabulary:

This activity has more children than that one.
There are fewer children painting than playing in the sand.
The groups of children are the same size.

▶ Repeat, changing the designated activities and the sizes of sets made.

Extension

▶ Repeat the activity using a larger number of faces, but again concentrating on visual comparison rather than counting.

② Does it match?

Learning objective	To make comparisons by direct matching.
Resources	• 10 coloured squares
Preparation	Divide the squares into 'heaps' of 6 and 4 on the board.

▶ Tell the children a story about a king who wanted to build a tall tower. He went to the builder who invited him to choose one of two piles of blocks to use.

Which pile of bricks should he choose?

▶ Allow the children to decide which pile of blocks looks the larger, and encourage them to check by seeing which pile would, in fact, build the tallest 'tower'.

▶ Build the towers side by side to allow direct comparison.

Which tower is the tallest?
Which is the tallest?
Which pile had more / less blocks?

▶ Repeat using block piles of different sizes.

▶ Finally include one large pile which can be chosen to build the king's tower.

③ Let's count them

Learning objective	To quantify comparisons by counting.
Resources	• number cards 1–10 • word cards 'is', 'more', 'less', 'than', and 'equals' • marker dots of assorted colours
Preparation	Draw two 'bag' shapes on the board, each about the size of a saucer.

▶ Tell the children that you are going to pretend to be a sweetshop keeper.

▶ The marker dots are going to be the sweets you sell. Encourage the children to tell you what their favourite types of sweets are, so that your shop will be popular! There are lots of bags of sweets in your shop.

▶ Without obviously counting them, place ten marker dots in one 'bag' and eight in the other.

▶ Ask the children which bag of sweets they would like to buy.

How do you know?

▶ Through discussion, decide with the children that the most reliable way of knowing which bag holds the most sweets is to count them. As you count the sweets from the first bag place them in a row on the board. Place those from the second bag, as you count them, directly underneath so that the sweets from the two bags are lined up in pairs.

▶ Point out that the row of ten sweets is longer than the row of eight. Build the sentences: 10 is more than 8; 8 is less than 10.

▶ Repeat using different numbers of sweets.

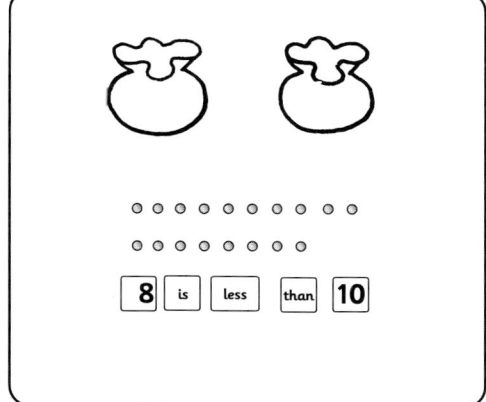

④ One more, one less

Learning objective	To make quantified comparisons of sets.
Resources	• number cards 1–10 • coloured squares • word cards 'is', 'more', 'less' and 'than'
Preparation	Make two rows of squares on the board, one of six squares and one of five.

▶ Tell the children that today they are going to be stationmasters. The two rows of squares are trains. Today there are going to be lots of passengers, so you need to use your longest train.

Which is the longest train?

▶ Encourage the children to count the number of sections in each train.

Which train has more sections?

▶ Use cards to make the sentences: 6 is more than 5; 5 is less than 6.

▶ Position the trains side by side so that direct comparisons can be made. Encourage the children to see that there is one additional section in the longer train.

▶ Compile the sentences: 6 is 1 more than 5; 5 is 1 less than 6.

▶ Now make a train of four sections, and invite a volunteer to make a train which has one section more. Again, consolidate by compiling number sentences.

Extension

▶ Make a set of three trains, with seven, eight and nine sections. What number sentences can be made now?

⑤ What's in the middle?

Learning objective	To develop an awareness of the order of numbers.
Resources	• picture cards 1–10 • number cards 1–10
Preparation	Draw three large circles in a row on the board.

▶ Distribute the picture and number cards amongst the children. Choose a child with a picture card with a large number of objects on it to come to the board. Show them how to put their card in the right-hand circle.

▶ Invite all the children to help to count the objects.

Who has that number card?

▶ The child with the correct number card places it beneath the picture.

▶ Next choose a child with a low number picture card, but this time show them how to place it in the left-hand circle. Again, the number card is placed beneath it. Point out that there is now a high number and a low number.

What could go in the middle?

▶ Talk about the numbers which might be suitable. Depending on the cards which are already on the board there may be more than one possibility.

▶ Encourage sentences about the cards used such as:

4 is bigger than 3 but smaller than 8.

▶ Collect all the cards, redistribute and repeat using different numbers.

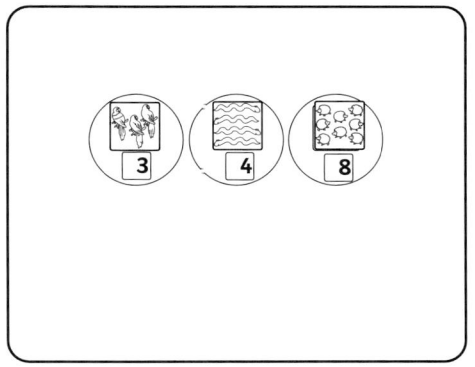

Unit 10: Number line puzzles

① Before and after, more and less

Learning objective	To consolidate the ordering of numbers 1–10.
Resources	• digit cards 1–10
Preparation	Draw a horizontal line across the middle of the board.

▶ Explain to the children that they are going to help you to build a number line. Start by placing the number 1 at the left-hand end of the line. Ask the children:

What number comes after 1? (2)

▶ Then continue by placing the number 10 at the right-hand end of the line.

What number comes before 10? (9)

▶ Continue to add numbers from alternate ends of the line until there is only one space left in the middle.

What number comes after 4 and before 6? (5)

▶ Depending on the confidence and experience of the children, you might decide at this point to build towers on each number as in the activity 'Number line towers', Unit 4.

▶ Develop the activity to include alternative vocabulary.

Who can show me a number which is 1 less than 7?

Who can show me a number which is 1 more than 8?

Extension

▶ Repeat the activity using numbers to 20.

② All mixed up

Learning objective	To consolidate the ordering of numbers 1–10.
Resources	• digit cards 0–10 • glove puppet (as in Units 1 and 4)
Preparation	Arrange the digit cards along a line across the board.

▶ Place the digit cards in random order at the top of the board. Explain to the children that the careless puppet wants to build a number line. Can they help her?

▶ Allow the children to give directions to the puppet, instructing her on the placement of the digit cards along the line.

▶ Now (after a whispered conversation) explain that the puppet wants to build a number line by herself to show to the children.

▶ Turn the board around and allow the puppet to build the number line, making a range of deliberate mistakes: numbers in exchanged places, several numbers out of sequence, individual numbers moved to the end of the line, etc.

▶ In each case allow the children to identify the mistakes, and to explain to the puppet how they should be rectified.

③ What's missing?

Learning objective	To consolidate the ordering of numbers 0–10.
Resources	• digit cards 0–10
Preparation	Draw a horizontal line across the middle of the board.

▶ Arrange the numbers, in order, along the line. Then remove the following numbers: 2, 3, 5, 7, 9.

▶ Explain to the children that when you were building the number line on the board you dropped some of the numbers. Can they help you to put them in place?

▶ Hold up each of the 'missing' digit cards in turn (in random order). Each time allow individuals to offer to place the number on the line. As each number is placed, talk about its positioning.

Why did you put the number there?

That's right – 3 comes before 4.

Why have you left a space next to the number?

Yes, there is another number to go in that space, isn't there?

Extension

▶ Repeat using numbers to 20.

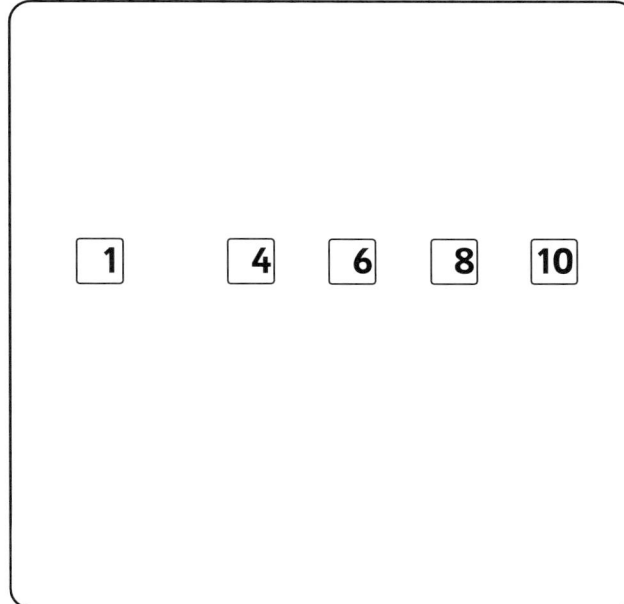

④ Put them in order

Learning objective	To develop the skill of ordering non-consecutive numbers.
Resources	• digit cards 0–10
Preparation	Draw a horizontal line across the middle of the board.

▶ Start building a number line by placing the cards in numerical order with the help of the children. Count along the line with the children.

Which are the larger numbers on the line?

Which are the smaller numbers on the line?

▶ Now remove the numbers, and place the numbers 5, 2, 9 and 7 on the board. Explain to the children that they are going to try to put these numbers in order, from the smallest to the largest.

Which is the smallest number? (2)

▶ Place the 2 at the left-hand side of the line.

▶ Now ask the children to look at the remaining three numbers.

Which is the smallest now? (5)

▶ Having placed the 5 next to the 2, draw attention to the 7 and 9 and repeat the question. Once the 9 has been added, the order of the numbers can be checked by counting to 10.

▶ Repeat using a different selection of numbers.

Extension

▶ Repeat the activity using a selection of non-consecutive number cards between 1 and 20.

⑤ I'm thinking of a number

Learning objective	To consolidate the ordering of numbers 1–10.
Resources	• digit cards 0–10
Preparation	Draw a horizontal line across the middle of the board. Use the cards to make a number line across the board.

▶ Tell the children that you are thinking about one of the numbers on the board. They have to guess which number you are thinking of. They can ask you any question they like to try to identify the number, but you will only answer 'Yes' or 'No'.

▶ At first the children will ask questions such as: 'Is it 6?' Each time the answer to a question is 'No', remove those numbers which have been 'eliminated from the enquiry'.

▶ Children soon discover that the most effective questions, which eliminate more numbers, are those such as 'Is it more that 5?'.

▶ Encourage children to keep a count of how many questions they used before they guessed the mystery number. Remind them that their best score will be the lowest number of questions!

Extension

▶ Extend the range from which you choose the mystery number. Allow children to take turns in choosing a number for others to guess.

Unit 11: Ordinal numbers

① The elephants queue

Learning objective	To introduce the vocabulary of ordinal numbers.
Resources	• 1 each: large red, blue, green and yellow elephant cards • 1 small red elephant card
Preparation	Arrange the elephants in a line with the small one at the front.

▶ Tell the children this story, moving the elephants as you go. Encourage audience participation in answering the ice-cream man's questions and joining in the repetitions.

It was hot day in the jungle, and the elephants were queuing to buy ice-creams. The baby red elephants was at the head of the queue, with four big elephant behind. The ice-cream man asked, 'Who is the first in the queue?'

And the little baby elephant was just about to say 'I am,' when the big elephant behind him rudely pushed in front and said, 'I am the first in the queue.'

Then the ice-cream man asked 'Who is the second in the queue?' And the little baby elephant was just about to say 'I am,' when the big elephant behind him rudely pushed in front and said, 'I am the second in the queue.'

Then the ice-cream man asked 'Who is the third in the queue?' And the little baby elephant was just about to say 'I am,' when the big elephant behind him rudely pushed in front and said, 'I am the third in the queue.'

Then the ice-cream man asked 'Who is the fourth in the queue?' And the little baby elephants was just about to say 'I am,' when the big elephant behind him rudely pushed in front and said: 'I am the fourth in the queue.'

Then the ice-cream man asked 'Who is the fifth in the queue?' And there were no more big elephants to push in front of the baby. The little baby elephant tearfully answered 'I am the fifth in the queue. I am the last.'

But the ice-cream man smiled and said, 'Never mind, I will save you the biggest ice-cream of all.'

② Sports day

Learning objective	To introduce the recording of ordinal numbers.
Resources	• ordinal number cards 1st–5th • 5 face cards

▶ Start by inviting the children to choose names for each of the faces so that they can be identified, and then use them to illustrate stories about an imaginary school sports day.

▶ After the first 'race', use the ordinal number cards as 'rosettes' to award to the participants. Draw attention to the letters on the cards. Say the names of the ordinal numbers carefully and invite the children to think about what these letters might mean. Spend some time exploring the idea that the letters represent the final sounds of the words.

▶ After each subsequent 'race' allow the children to identify the ordinal number cards.

Carrie came first. Which rosette card should we give her? (1st)

Extension

▶ Extend the ordinal numbers introduced to 'tenth'.

③ Ordinal quiz

Learning objective	To develop familiarity with the use of ordinal numbers.
Resources	• 10 face cards • ordinal number cards 1st–5th
Preparation	Arrange 5 of the faces across the board.

▶ With help from the children, use the ordinal number cards to label each face in the line on the board. Now ask a series of questions, encouraging children to answer using the ordinal number names. For example:

Which faces have their hair in bunches?
Which faces are wearing glasses?
Which faces are not smiling?
Which faces have blond hair?

▶ Every now and then use the remaining five face cards to make changes in the line, allowing the game to continue for longer.

Extension

▶ Try removing the ordinal number cards. Explain to the children that they will now need to identify the ordinal numbers by counting.

④ Find the ruby

Learning objective	To introduce and use ordinal numbers to tenth.
Resources	• coloured squares of mixed colours • ordinal number cards 1st–10th • red marker dot
Preparation	Arrange the ordinal number cards randomly at the bottom of the board.

▶ Use ten of the coloured squares to make a multicoloured row across the board. Leave about a card's width between each one, to allow space for labelling.

▶ Introduce the children to the number cards 6th–10th, drawing attention to the 'th' letters which represent the final sounds of the ordinal number words.

▶ Invite children to match the ordinal number cards to the coloured squares.

Can you label the third square in the row?

Can you label the ninth square in the row?

▶ Continue until all the ordinal number cards have been used.

▶ Now return the ordinal number cards to the bottom of the board. Explain that you are going to hide a precious jewel, called a ruby, behind one of the squares. Show the children the red 'ruby' marker dot, and then hide it, without them seeing, behind one of the coloured squares.

▶ Invite the children to try to identify the hiding place. First they must identify the square they wish to search, then place the corresponding ordinal number card beneath it. Continue until the ruby is found.

▶ Repeat several times.

⑤ What will it be?

Learning objective	To make predictions about pattern using ordinal numbers.
Resources	• coloured squares
Preparation	Use eight squares to make a simple repeating pattern across the board, for example: red, red, blue, blue, red, red, blue, blue.

▶ Start by asking children to point to the third, fourth, seventh squares, etc. in the pattern. Then continue the activity by asking children to make predictions.

If I carried on this pattern what colour would the ninth square be?

And the tenth?

▶ Change the pattern and repeat.

Extension

▶ Invite children to make their own patterns on the board for others to use in making predictions.

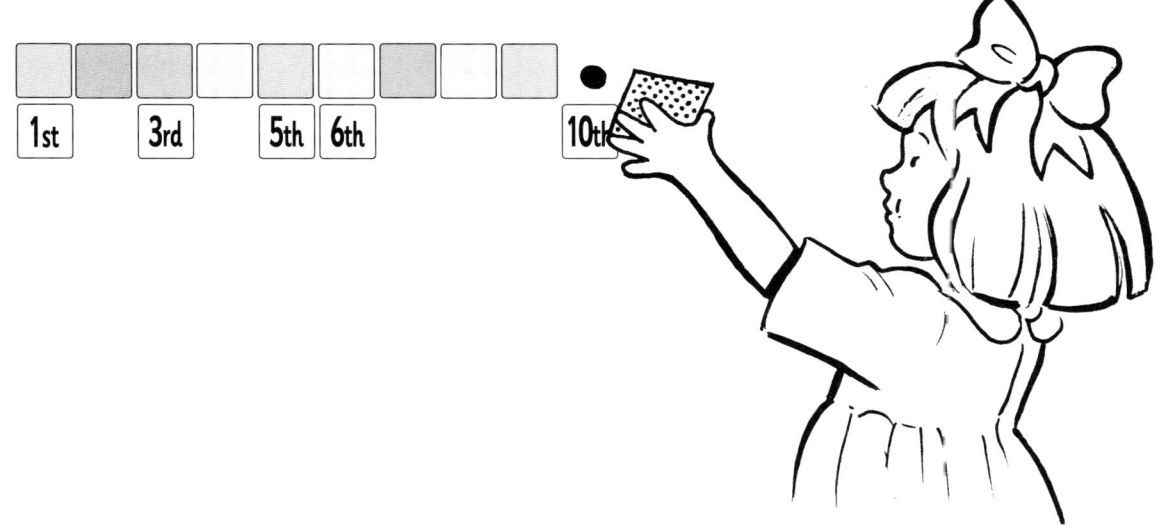

1st 3rd 5th 6th 10th

Unit 12: Addition 1 – combining sets

① How many now?

Learning objective	To introduce the vocabulary of addition.
Resources	• 10 face cards • word card 'altogether'

▶ Place three of the face cards on the board. Explain to the children that these are three friends who are playing together.

▶ Show the children one more face card and explain that this is another friend who is going to join in the game.

How many children will be playing together now? (4)

▶ Add the extra face to the group on the board and encourage the children to count the complete group. Talk about the process. Explain that you have 'added' a new friend to the group. Repeat the operation in words:

There were three children and you added one more.
Now there are four children altogether.

▶ Show the children the word card 'altogether' to reinforce the vocabulary.

▶ Repeat, progressing to numbers beyond five as the children become more confident.

② The elephant walk

Learning objective	To introduce addition sentences.
Resources	• 10 elephant cards

▶ Place one elephant card near to the left-hand side of the board. Tell the children that this elephant is going for a walk in the jungle. Encourage the children to imagine the scene.

It is a lovely day and before long another elephant decides to join him.

▶ Explain how elephants like to walk in a line, each holding the tail of the one in front.

How many elephants are there altogether now?

▶ Introduce the spoken addition sentences:

One elephant and one more makes two.
One add one makes two.

▶ Spend some time introducing the word 'add'. Children may have come across it in hearing recipes.

What do we mean by 'add an egg' in a recipe?

▶ Explain that when we talk about 'adding' things, we mean 'put them together'.

▶ Now another elephant joins the walk:

How many elephants were there before this one joined?
How many are there altogether now?
Two elephants and one more makes three.
Two add one makes three.

▶ Repeat until there are ten elephants in the line.

Extension

▶ Repeat the activity adding groups of two elephants.

③ Put them together

Learning objective	To develop the understanding of addition as the combining of sets.
Resources	• 10 face cards • addition overlay • word card 'altogether'

▶ Place sets of one and two face cards in the overlay as shown.

▶ With the children, count the numbers of faces in each set.

How many would there be if all these children played together? (3)

▶ Move all the face cards together into the large, lower region. Explain that you are going to bring or 'add' the faces altogether and emphasise the physical process of doing this.

How many are there now altogether? (3)

▶ Place the word card 'altogether' near to the larger region to emphasise the vocabulary.

One and two make three altogether.

or

One add two makes three.

▶ Repeat using a variety of combinations with a maximum total of 5, extending to 10 as children gain confidence.

Extension

▶ What happens when one of the initial two sets has no faces in it? How would children describe the addition?

④ Add the squares

Learning objective	To introduce the notation of addition.
Resources	• number cards 1–10 • addition sign card • equals sign card • 10 coloured squares • addition overlay • word cards 'add', 'equals', 'plus'

▶ Explain to the children that together you are going to do some more adding, but this time you are going to show them how 'adding' sums are sometimes written down.

▶ Start by placing sets of two and three squares in the small circles of the addition overlay. Count them with the children and then describe how you are bringing or 'adding' the squares together as you move both sets into the larger region.

How many squares are there now altogether? (5)

▶ Encourage children to put the process into words:

Two and three make five.

or

Two add three makes five.

▶ Show the children the addition sign card and explain that it stands for the word 'add'. It is also called a 'plus' sign.

▶ Use the number and operations cards to show 2 + 3. Explain that this means two add three, or two plus three.

▶ Replace the '+' sign, in turn, with the word cards 'add' and 'plus' to reinforce this.

▶ Now show the children the equals sign card.

Does anyone know what this card means?

▶ Explain that this sign is called an equals sign and it means 'makes'. Add the equals sign to the number sentence on the board.

So 2 + 3 = 5 means 'two add three makes five', or 'two plus three equals five'.

▶ Reinforce the new vocabulary by compiling the number sentence again, this time replacing the addition sign and equals sign cards with the word cards 'plus' and 'equals'.

▶ Return to the overlay and repeat, using initial sets totalling no more than 5, extending to 10 as children gain confidence.

⑤ What's the number?

Learning objective	To begin to carry out the addition of numbers with apparatus support.
Resources	• number cards 1–9 • addition sign card • equals sign card • 10 coloured squares • addition overlay • word cards 'plus', 'equals'

▶ Explain to the children that they are going to use the number cards to tell them the addition sum to solve.

▶ Place the cards 1–5 on the board and invite children to choose two numbers.

▶ Allow individuals to help you to use the chosen number cards, together with the addition sign card and the equals sign card, to make an addition sum at the bottom of the board. Now that we have the sum, how are we going to work out the answer?

▶ Encourage them to decide for themselves that it would be helpful to use the squares to support them in carrying out the number operation. Place the appropriate numbers of coloured squares in the two small regions. Bring the squares together into the larger region and ask the children:

How many squares are there now altogether?

Which number card do we need now?

▶ Use the appropriate number card to complete the sum on the board. Reinforce by compiling the number sentence again, replacing the addition sign and the equals sign cards with the word cards 'plus' and 'equals'.

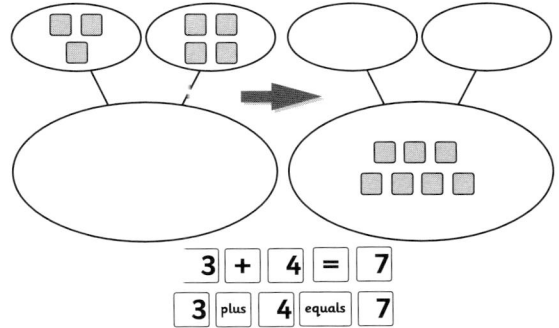

Unit 13: Addition 2 – counting on

① Stepping stones

Learning objective	To develop the concept of counting on along a number line.
Resources	• 1 monkey card • digit cards 1–10 • additional digit cards 1–5 • word cards 'count' and 'on'
Preparation	Draw a line down each side of the board. Between these lines draw a series of ten 'stepping stones'.

▶ Explain to the children that the lines down the sides of the board are the banks of the great jungle river. The only way to cross the river is to use the stepping stones.

▶ Count the stepping stones with the children labelling each with a digit card (1–10) from left to right across the board.

▶ Now introduce the monkey, placing the card on the river bank at the left of the board. He is very playful, and loves to jump between the stones as he crosses the river. Show the children how the monkey can jump by making two jumps to the stone labelled 2.

▶ Now invite a child to choose a digit card from 1–5 from your hand. The monkey can 'count on' this many jumps. Remind the children that the monkey is jumping towards the other bank of the river.

Which stone will he land on now?

▶ Now revise the completed process. Remind the children that the monkey started on stone number 2.

How many jumps did the monkey 'count on'?
Which stone is he on now?

▶ Record the process using the digit and word cards with an arrow between.

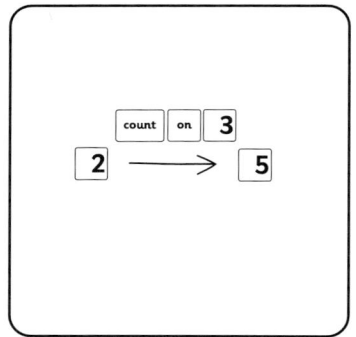

▶ Repeat, allowing children to choose digit cards 1–5 to decide which stone the monkey starts on and how many jumps he makes.

Extension

▶ How many jumps would it take the monkey to reach the other river bank?

② Count on us!

Learning objective	To introduce the idea of 'counting on' from an existing number.
Resources	• face cards

▶ Place four face cards on the board in a horizontal row. Count them, emphasising the final count: one, two, three, four.

▶ Now add another three faces to the row.

How many faces are there now? (7)

▶ Talk to the children about how they could work this out.

But do we really need to count the whole group?

▶ Point out that the original group of four has not moved. Put your finger back on the face which was number 4.

▶ Now count on along the complete group: 4, 5, 6, 7. Explain to the children that you are 'counting on'.

▶ Repeat the activity using different small numbers.

▶ Each time emphasise the process of counting on from the final member of the original group to determine the new size of the set.

③ The monkey line

Learning objective	To introduce counting on along a number line as addition.
Resources	• 10 monkey cards • number line overlay • digit cards 0–10 • additional digit cards 0–10 • addition sign card • equals sign card
Preparation	Place the number line on the board, with the digit cards in position below it.

▶ Explain to the children that they are going to use the number line to help them to do some addition sums. Some of the playful monkeys are going to help them.

Here is a sum for us to do.

▶ Use the digit and operations cards and the equals sign card to place the incomplete sum 3 + 2 = on the board.

How could the monkeys help us?

▶ Three of the monkeys offer to sit on the number line. Place them in the spaces at the left of the line.

Count the monkeys with the children, pointing to the numerals. Now look back to the sum.

What does the sum ask us to do? It asks us to add two more monkeys.

▶ Add the two additional monkeys to the line, occupying the spaces 4 and 5.

How many monkeys are there now? Look at the number line to help you.

The number line has helped us to count on. We had three monkeys on the line. One, two, three, (hold finger on number three) then added two more: four, five.

▶ Complete the recording of the sum 3 + 2 = 5.

▶ Repeat using different numbers with a maximum total of 10.

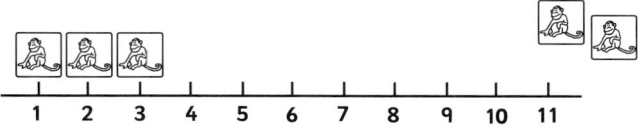

④ The adding frog

Learning objective	To develop the skill of addition as counting on along a number line.
Resources	• number line overlay • number cards 1–10 • green square • word cards 'plus' and 'equals' • addition sign card • equals sign card
Preparation	Place the numerals in position along the number line.

▶ Explain to the children that this time they are going to use the jumping frog to help them to do some adding sums. Introduce the 'frog' represented by the green square.

▶ Use cards to place the incomplete sum 4 + 3 = on the board.

Where should the green frog start his jumps?

▶ Ensure that the children understand that the frog should be placed on the number 4 as that is the start of the sum.

How many are we adding on? (3)
How many jumps should the frog take? (3)

▶ As the frog takes his three jumps to the right, it is useful to demonstrate how to keep a finger held in the starting place. Again, stress the importance of 'one count – one move'.

▶ When the three jumps are taken ask:

Which square is the frog on now? (7)
So four plus three is? (7)
That's right. We counted on three jumps. Four add three equals seven.

▶ Invite a child to find the numeral 7 to complete the sum on the board.

Extension

▶ As the children become more confident increase the number of jumps needed, e.g. 2 + 8 =

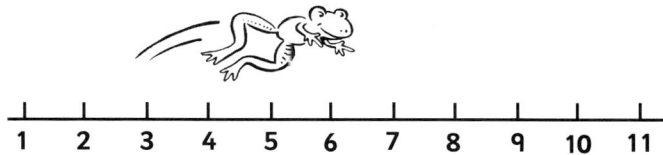

⑤ The Minibeasts' Ball

Learning objective	To count on as a means of addition using larger numbers.
Resources	• 10 red marker dots • 10 green marker dots • number cards 1–20 • addition sign card • equals sign card

▶ The red and green marker dots represent the guests at the Minibeasts' Ball. There are red ladybirds and green grasshoppers. As the band strikes up a group of ladybirds are the first to take to the floor!

▶ Make a row of seven red spots.

How many ladybirds are there? (7)

▶ Now add six green spots to the line as they are joined by dancing grasshoppers.

How many minibeasts are dancing now? (13)

▶ Remind the children that they do not need to count the whole line from the beginning, but can count on from 7 as we know there were 7 ladybirds. Record the sum as 6 + 7 = 13.

▶ Repeat using different numbers to a maximum total of 20.

Extension

▶ What would the sum be if all the ladybirds were dancing, and each had a grasshopper partner? Use the spots to help.

Unit 14: Using addition

① Monkey teams

Learning objective	To discover the number bonds to 5.
Resources	• digit cards 0–5 • 5 red monkeys • 5 blue monkeys • marker pen
Preparation	Place the monkeys in alternate colours in a row at the top of the board. At the bottom of the board make a recording chart.

▶ It is sports day in the jungle. The monkeys are getting ready to play in the five-a-side football competition. They need to make a team of five players.

Red	Blue

But how many red monkeys and how many blue monkeys could be in the team?

▶ Invite the children to help you to make up a team of five monkeys chosen from the top of the board.

How many red monkeys are in the team?
How many blue?
How many monkeys are in the team altogether?

▶ Record the numbers of red and blue monkeys on the chart using a marker pen.

Can we make a different team?

▶ Continue the activity, collecting all the number bonds to 5. Remind the children that the team could be all one colour!

② Tightrope monkeys

Learning objective	To explore number bonds to 10.
Resources	• 10 monkey cards • marker pen
Preparation	Draw a simple wide platform at either side of the board, with a tightrope between.

▶ Today these monkeys are playing at walking along a tightrope. They are wonderful at balancing!

How many monkeys are there?

▶ Put all ten monkey cards in a heap on one of the platforms. Some of the monkeys are going to balance along the rope. Invite children to move some of the monkey cards across to the other platform.

How many monkeys are on each platform?

▶ Summarise by saying:

There are six monkeys on one platform and four on the other. There are ten monkeys altogether.

▶ Record: 6 + 4 = 10 at the bottom of the board.

▶ Continue the game, allowing children to move monkeys between the platforms, each time recording the numbers on each. Remind the children that there are always ten monkeys altogether.

How many different sums can the children make and record?

Extension

▶ Discuss whether or not 6 + 4 is the same as 4 + 6.

③ The jungle bus

Learning objective	To consolidate number bonds to 10.
Resources	• 10 mixed elephant and monkey cards • marker pen
Preparation	Draw ten sections, each approximately 10 x 5 cm on the board.

▶ Place the ten animals at the top of the board. Explain to the children that this is the jungle bus. It has ten seats on it. Each box that they can see on the board is a seat on the bus.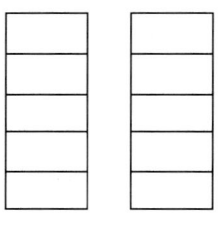

▶ Point out the queue of animals waiting to get on the bus.

How many animals are there? (10)

▶ At the first bus stop one animal gets on the bus.

How many more animals could get on to fill all ten seats? (9)

▶ Record as 1 + 9 = 10.

▶ Continue the story, adding one more animal at each bus stop. Gradually build up all the number bonds to 10. For example:

1 + 9 = 10
2 + 8 = 10
3 + 7 = 10 and so on.

What would be the sum recorded when the bus was empty? (0 + 10 = 10) or full? (10 + 0 = 10)

Extension

▶ Look at the number patterns in the collected number bonds. The first number in the sum increases by one as the children look down the list, and the second number decreases by one.

 **Join up!**

Learning objective	To add three numbers together.
Resources	• 3 each: red, green and blue coloured squares. • 3 sets numbers 1–3 • 1 set numbers 1–9 • 2 addition sign cards • equals sign card

▶ Explain to the children that today they are going to add three numbers together. Invite three individuals to each choose a number: 1, 2 or 3.

▶ Make sets of the three colours of squares using these chosen numbers. For example: two red, one green and three blue squares. Remind the children that addition is about bringing things together.

▶ Explain that an addition sum is rather like a recipe. When we are cooking things we don't just throw everything together, we add things a bit at a time.

So, we are going to add the things in the sum a bit at a time.

▶ Encourage the children to look at the first part of the sum: 2 + 1.

The answer to this bit of the sum is 3. What does the sum ask us to add next?
That's right, add 3. So the sum we are doing now is 3 + 3.

▶ Check the final answer by counting the six squares. Record the sum using the number and operations cards and the equals sign card: 2 + 1 + 3 = 6.

▶ Repeat using different numbers from each group of squares.

Extension

▶ Increase the size of each group of squares to 5 to allow for totals greater than 10.

⑤ Baby elephants's birthday

Learning objective	To carry out addition when the objects are hidden.
Resources	• small elephant card • 10 coloured squares • piece of coloured A4 paper
Preparation	Hold the paper against the board using one or two additional coloured squares.

▶ Tell the children this story:

It will soon be Baby Elephant's birthday. He is getting very excited!
The paper held against the board is Mrs Elephant's cupboard. This is where she hides the presents ready for his birthday.
Mrs Elephant has bought two presents and she hides them in her cupboard.

▶ Place two coloured squares behind the coloured paper.

Can you remember how many parcels are in the cupboard? Keep thinking about them!

The jungle postman knocks on the door. He has brought another parcel for Baby Elephant. Mrs Elephant puts this parcel with the others in her special cupboard.

▶ If necessary turn the board around whilst you place one more square behind the piece of paper.

How many parcels are there in the cupboard for Baby Elephant's birthday?

▶ Encourage the children to visualise the original two parcels, and the one new addition. Then 'open' the cupboard to check the answer.

▶ Having established that there are now three parcels, repeat the process as other jungle visitors add to the growing collection – sometimes bringing two or three presents. Continue until there are ten parcels in the cupboard. Finally, allow the children to enjoy predicting what might be inside the parcels for Baby Elephant.

Extension

▶ Add more than one set of parcels between checks inside the cupboard.

Unit 15: Subtraction 1 – partitioning sets

① How many left?

Learning objective	To introduce the vocabulary of subtraction.
Resources	• 10 face cards

▶ Place a row of five face cards on the board. Explain to the children that these are children at school and that it is going home time. Count the faces with the children.

▶ Remove one of the faces, explaining that this child has now gone home.

▶ Encourage the children to count the number of faces left.

One child has gone home. How many are left? (4)

▶ Talk about the process.

There were five children and we took one away.
There are four children left.

▶ Repeat the activity encouraging the children to make sentences describing what has happened after each 'face' leaves.

Extension

▶ Increase the number of faces on the board to ten. Remove faces two or three at a time, again encouraging children to verbalise the process.

② Back on the elephant bus

Learning objective	To introduce subtraction sentences.
Resources	• 10 elephant cards
Preparation	Draw ten sections on the board, each approximately 10 x 5 cm.

▶ Place one elephant card in each of the sections on the board. Explain to the children that the board shows ten elephants travelling home on the jungle bus.

How many elephants are on the bus? (10)

▶ The bus reaches a stop and one elephant gets off the bus.

How many elephants are left on the bus? (9)

▶ Introduce the spoken subtraction sentences:

Ten elephants take away one is nine.
Ten take away one is nine.

▶ Explain that there are other words which mean the same as 'take away'. These words are 'subtract' and 'minus'.

Ten subtract one is nine.
Ten minus one is nine.

▶ At the next stop two elephants get off.

How many elephants are left on the bus now?
Nine take away two is seven.
Nine subtract two is seven.
Nine minus two is seven.

▶ Repeat until the bus is empty.

③ Split them up

Learning objective	To introduce subtraction as the partitioning of a set.
Resources	• 10 face cards • addition / subtraction overlay • word cards 'one', 'two', 'three', 'four', 'five', 'is', 'take away', 'minus', 'subtract'
Preparation	Place the overlay on the board with the larger region uppermost.

▶ Place three face cards in the overlay as shown.

▶ Explain to the children that these are a group of three friends playing together. With the children count the number of faces in the set.

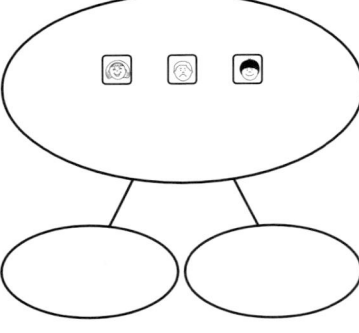

How many would there be if one of the friends left the set?

▶ Move one of the faces into the right-hand smaller region. Explain that you are 'taking away' one of the faces.

How many friends are still playing together?

▶ Place the word card 'take away' next to the line which joins the larger circle to the right-hand smaller circle.

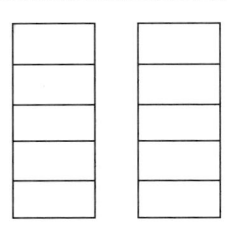

38

▶ Make the following sentence on the board, using cards, and encourage the children to read it with you:

Three take away one is two.

▶ Replace the card 'take away' with the word card 'minus' and say:

Three minus one is two.

▶ Finally replace the card 'minus' with the word card 'subtract' and say:

Three subtract one is two.

▶ Repeat starting with any number to 5 from the original set.

Extension

▶ As children become more confident, increase the number of children in the original set to ten.

④ Taking away squares

Learning objective	To introduce the notation of subtraction.
Resources	• addition / subtraction overlay • 2 sets of digit cards 0–10 • subtraction sign card • equals sign card • word cards 'take away', 'subtract', 'minus' and 'equals' • 10 coloured squares
Preparation	Place the overlay on the board with the larger region uppermost.

▶ Explain to the children that you are going to show them how 'taking away' sums are sometimes written down.

▶ Start by placing five squares in the larger region of the overlay. Count them with the children and explain how you are taking two squares away as you move them to the lower right region.

▶ Encourage the children to put the process into words:

Five take away two is three.
Five minus two is three.
Five subtract two is three.

▶ Show the children the subtraction sign card and explain that this is called a 'minus' sign. It means that you are being asked to take something away.

▶ Use the digit cards to show 5 – 2. Replace the subtraction sign card in turn with the words 'take away' and 'minus', each time reading the number phrase to the children.

▶ Now include the equals sign card to make the phrase 5 – 2 = 3. Beneath it use words and numerals together to make the sentences:

5 take away 2 equals 3.
5 minus 2 equals 3.

▶ Return to the overlay and repeat using starting sets of no more than five, extending to ten as children become more confident.

⑤ Pick two numbers

Learning objective	To begin to carry out the subtraction of numbers with the support of apparatus.
Resources	• digit cards 0–10 • subtraction sign card • equals sign card • word cards 'minus' and 'equals' • 10 coloured squares • addition / subtraction overlay
Preparation	Place the overlay on the board with the larger region uppermost. Divide the digit cards into two sets at the top of the board: 0–5 and 6–10.

▶ Explain to the children that they are going to use the digit cards to make taking away sums to solve.

▶ Allow an individual to choose a card from the 6–10 set. This will be the first number in the sum. Place this digit card at the bottom of the board. Then place a subtraction sign card next to it.

▶ Now a card is chosen from the 0–5 set. Use this card, with the equals sign card, to make a subtraction sum at the bottom of the board.

Now that we have the sum, how are we going to find the answer?

▶ Encourage children to decide for themselves that it would be helpful to use the squares as support.

▶ Place the appropriate number of coloured squares in the large region of the overlay. Move the smaller number of squares into the small right-hand region.

▶ Use the appropriate number card to complete the sum at the bottom of the board. Reinforce by compiling the number sentence again, replacing the subtraction sign card and the equals sign card with the words cards 'minus' and 'equals'.

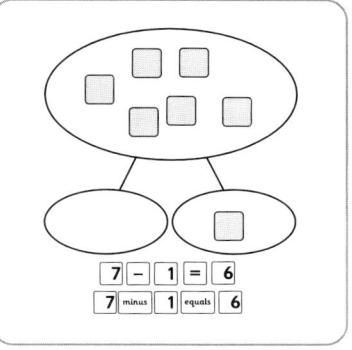

7 – 1 = 6
7 minus 1 equals 6

Unit 16: Subtraction 2 – counting back

① Counting back

Learning objective	To become familiar with the sequence of numbers when counting back.
Resources	• 10 monkey cards • number cards 1–10

▶ Place the monkey cards one at a time on the board, building a line from left to right across the board. As each monkey is added to the line invite children to place the appropriate numerals beneath them.

▶ Say the following action rhyme with the children:

Ten little monkeys bouncing on the bed
　　　(with fingers upright hands
　　　are moved up and down)
One fell off and bumped his head
　　　(clutch hand to forehead)
Mummy phoned the doctor
　　　(hold imaginary phone to ear,
　　　dialling with other hand)
and the doctor said:
'No more monkeys bouncing on the bed!'
　　　(wag finger and adopt very
　　　cross voice)

Next verse:

Nine little monkeys …
　　　(nine 'bouncing' fingers)

and so on …

▶ As each verse is completed ask the question: 'How many are left?' Remove one monkey card and its corresponding numeral from the board.

▶ Repeat, starting with a row of monkeys but no number cards. After each verse invite children to find the number card which shows the number of monkeys remaining.

② Count back swing

Learning objective	To develop the concept of counting back along a number line.
Resources	• 1 monkey card • number cards 1–10 • additional numbers 1–5 • word cards 'count' and 'back' • marker pen
Preparation	Draw ten bushy trees in an approximately horizontal line across the board.

▶ Explain to the children that monkeys love to swing from tree to tree in the jungle.

How many trees are there on the board? (10)

▶ Invite children to help you to number the trees with number cards from left to right.

▶ Introduce the monkey who is going to swing from tree to tree starting from tree number 10. Point out that as the monkey swings he will be counting back.

▶ Invite a child to choose a number card from 1–5. The monkey can 'count back' this many swings.

Which tree will he land in?

▶ Remind the children that the monkey started in tree 10.

How many swings did he count back?
Which tree is he in now?

▶ Record the process using the number and word cards with an arrow between.

▶ Repeat, each time starting the monkey in a tree numbered from 6–10, and allowing children to choose number cards from 1–5 to decide how many swings he will take.

Extension

▶ Ask questions:

How many swings would the monkey take to reach tree 1?

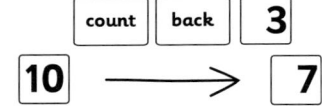

③ The elephant line

Learning objective	To introduce counting back along a number line as subtraction.
Resources	• 10 elephant cards • number line overlay • digit cards 0–10 • additional digit cards 0–10 • subtraction sign card • equals sign card
Preparation	Place the number line on the board with the digit cards in position below it.

▶ Explain to the children that they are going to use the number line to help them to do some taking away sums. Some of the elephants are going to help them.

Here is a sum for us to do:

▶ Use the digit and operations cards and the equals sign card to place the problem 5 – 3 = on the board.

Read the sum to the children:

What is 5 take away 3? 5 minus 3 equals?

How could the elephants help us?

▶ Place five elephant cards on the number line, occupying spaces 1–5.

What does the sum ask us to do?

It asks us to take away three elephants.

▶ Show the children how to count three elephants from the right-hand end of the line. Point out that this is a counting back process. Count back three spaces reaching the number 2 on the number line.

▶ Remove the three elephants counted and draw attention to the two remaining.

One way of 'taking away' is to count back along the number line.

▶ Complete the sum by adding the digit and operations cards and the equals sign card: 5 – 3 = 2.

▶ Repeat, subtracting from numbers up to 10.

④ Take it away grasshopper!

Learning objective	To develop the skills of subtraction as counting back along a number line.
Resources	• number line overlay • number cards 1–10 • subtraction sign card • equals sign card • green square
Preparation	Place the numerals in sequence along the number line.

▶ Introduce the green square as the 'taking away grasshopper'. He loves to help children to do taking away sums. He helps by jumping backwards, or 'counting back' along number lines.

▶ Use the number and operations cards and the equals sign card to place the problem 5 – 4 = on the board.

Where should grasshopper start his jumps? On the 5 or the 4?

▶ Ensure that the children understand that the grasshopper should be placed on 5 as that is the start of the sum.

How many does the sum ask us to take away?

So how many spaces should grasshopper count back?

▶ As the grasshopper takes his four jumps to the left, it is useful to demonstrate how to keep a finger held in the starting place. Again, stress the importance of 'one count – one move'.

▶ When the four jumps are taken ask:

Which number is grasshopper on now?

So five take away four is ...?

That's right. We counted back four jumps.

Five take away, or minus, four equals one.

▶ Remind the children that these problems might also be phrased as 'five minus four', or 'five subtract four'. Whichever words are used to describe a taking away sum, counting back will sort it out!

Extension

▶ As the children gain confidence increase the number of jumps needed, e.g. 10 – 7 =

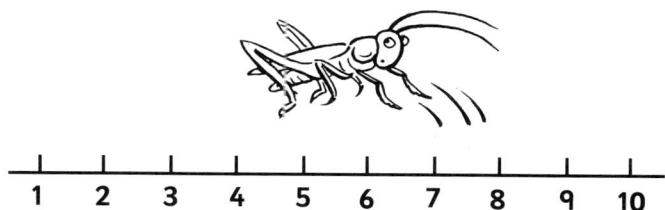

1	2	3	4	5	6	7	8	9	10

⑤ Going bananas!

Learning objective	To count back as a means of subtraction using larger numbers.
Resources	• 20 yellow marker dots • 1 monkey card • number cards 1–20 • subtraction sign card • equals sign card

▶ Use the number cards from 1–20 to make a wavy number line on the board, rather like a 'number snake'.

▶ Above each number card place a yellow marker dot.

▶ Tell the children that these are delicious bananas. Then introduce the hungry monkey.

How many bananas do the children think he might eat?

▶ Encourage the children to choose a number between 10 and 20, e.g. the children decide that the monkey will eat 14 bananas.

How many will be left?

The sum would be twenty take away fourteen. (6)

▶ This seems a very difficult sum to work out, but remind the children that an easy way to do a take away sum is to count back along a number line.

▶ Choose a volunteer to count back fourteen places starting from twenty.

▶ Once the answer is discovered record the sum using the number and operations cards and the equals sign card: 20 – 14 = 6.

Unit 17: More calculation

① How many have gone?

Learning objective	To find how many objects have been removed from a set by counting up from the remainder.
Resources	• 10 green squares • number line • number cards 1–10
Preparation	Place the numerals under the number line in sequence.

▶ Place five green squares on the number line in positions 1–5. Explain that these are frogs who live in a pond. Count the frogs with the children.

▶ Turn the board away from the children, and tell them that the frogs are very lively and quite often like to jump right out of the pond! Before turning the board back, remove the two frogs from spaces 4 and 5. Turn the board back and ask:

Are there still five frogs in the pond?

Oh no! Some of them have jumped out!

How many are left?

How can we work out how many have gone?

▶ Point to 5 on the number line.

This is where the frog line was before.

▶ Now return to the remaining frogs and count them: 1, 2, 3, ...

Continue to count to 5, raising fingers on counts 4 and 5 to show that you are counting the empty spaces.

▶ Allow the disappearing frogs to return and then repeat with a different number of escapees!

Extension

▶ Progress to starting with ten frogs, with increasing numbers missing.

② How many more?

Learning objective	To calculate how many more are needed to make a larger number.
Resources	• 10 red squares • number line • number cards 1–10
Preparation	Place the number line across the board with the numerals in position beneath it.

▶ Tell the children a story about a little boy who was collecting tokens from the inside of chocolate bar wrappers. When he had ten tokens he would be able to exchange them for a toy spaceship at the shop.

▶ He starts the collection with one token. Place the one red token at the left-hand end of the number line.

How many more does he need to reach 10? (9)

▶ Encourage the children to decide for themselves that one way to find out is to count the still-empty spaces along the number line to 10.

▶ Count up from 1. As you say the names of the empty squares show the children how to make fists, and then raise one finger for each count: 2, 3, 4, 5, 6, 7, 8, 9, 10.

How many fingers are raised? (9)

How many empty squares are there? (9)

How many more tokens are needed? (1)

▶ Continue the story, allowing the boy to find more tokens, sometimes in unexpected places, until the wonderful day is reached when he is able to get his spaceship.

Extension

▶ Twenty tokens can be exchanged for an intergalactic space station. Continue the story, sometimes including the finding of several tokens at once.

③ Take your partners

Learning objective	To find the difference between a larger and smaller number by counting back or counting up.
Resources	• 10 elephant cards • 10 monkey cards

▶ Today the elephants and monkeys are at a jungle dancing class. They are learning to do a special dance. Each elephant must have a monkey partner, but there is a problem. The naughty monkeys keep running away.

▶ Make a vertical line of five elephants on the board.

▶ Tell the children that the dancing teacher is calling the monkeys to join their partners.

▶ Place four monkeys on the board, partnering all except the uppermost elephant.

Are there enough monkeys? (No)

How many elephants are there? (5)

How many monkeys are there? (4)

How many elephants have no partner? (1)

▶ Introduce the idea that we are looking at the difference between the number of elephants and the number of monkeys.

The difference between 5 and 4 is 1.

▶ Place the necessary monkey in position and then repeat the activity. Each time start with five elephants and a different, smaller number of monkeys.

Extension

▶ Increase the number of dancing elephants to 10.

④ Back to bonds

Learning objective	To reinforce number bonds to 5.
Resources	• 5 monkey cards • marker pen
Preparation	Draw a large tree on the board. Draw a line from the branches of the tree down to the bottom of the board.

▶ Place the five monkey cards in the tree top. Explain to the children that today the monkeys are playing with a rope. They are taking it in turns to slide down the rope to the ground.

▶ Slide one monkey card down the rope to the ground and remove it from the board.

We had five monkeys and one went away.

How many are left?

▶ Record the sum as 5 – 1 = 4 at one side of the board.

▶ Take the opportunity to revisit vocabulary, reminding children of the words 'take away', 'subtract', 'minus' and 'equals'.

▶ Repeat, removing one monkey at a time until no monkeys are left in the tree. Record each number story as a sum, adding to a list on the board.

Extension

▶ Can the children make a take away number sentence for the beginning of the story? (5 – 0 = 5)

⑤ Greedy monkey!

Learning objective	To develop skills of imagery as subtraction is carried out with hidden objects.
Resources	• 1 monkey card • 5 yellow squares • 2 additional coloured squares of another colour • a piece of A4 paper

Mrs Monkey has been baking. She has made five lovely banana cakes for the monkey family's tea.

▶ Show the children the five yellow cards to represent the banana cakes.

Mrs Monkey puts the banana cakes on a rack and covers them with a cloth to cool. Then she goes outside to chat to a neighbour.

▶ Put the five yellow cards on the board. Cover them with the piece of paper held in place by the two extra squares. Introduce the monkey card.

This is little Miss Monkey. Little Miss Monkey smells the delicious banana cakes and follows the smell with her nose. She finds the cakes hidden under the cloth.

▶ Turn the board away from the children.

Whilst no-one is looking Little Miss Monkey takes one banana cake from the tray. It tastes wonderful!

▶ Remind the children that there were five cakes and one has now gone.

How many cakes are left under the cloth? (4)

▶ Turn the board back and allow the children to look under the cloth to check. Then continue the story, as Little Miss Monkey takes all the cakes, one at a time. After each removal allow prediction and checking of the number of cakes left.

When Mrs Monkey returns from the garden she sees that all the cakes are gone, and Little Miss Monkey is fast asleep under the table with a very full tummy!

Extension

▶ Start with ten cakes, occasionally removing more than one at a time.

Unit 18: Halves and doubles

① Monkey twins

Learning objective	To introduce doubles.
Resources	• 2 monkey cards of the same colour • marker dots of assorted colours • marker pen

▶ Introduce the children to the monkey twins.

They are exactly alike in every way. They are doubles.

▶ Use the twins as a context for exploring doubles.

How many tails does one monkey have?
How many do the twins have?
Double one is two.

How many eyes does one monkey have?
How many do the twins have?
Double two is four.

▶ Continue to use body parts or possessions (represented by marker dots), until you reach double five.

▶ Enjoy this action rhyme:

Double one is two
Tap it with your shoe.

Double two is four
Wriggle on the floor.

Double three is six
Make some finger clicks.

Double four is eight
Stretch your arms up straight.

Double five is ten
Let's begin again.

② Making doubles

Learning objective	To reinforce the concept of doubles.
Resources	• picture cards 1–5 • marker dots of assorted colours • number cards 2, 4, 6, 8, 10

▶ Place the one giraffe picture card on the board.

How many things are on the card?

▶ Invite a volunteer to place the same number (in this case 1) of marker dots beneath the picture. Underneath the picture and dot write the phrase 'Double 1 is …'

▶ Invite a volunteer to add the correct number card to record the double.

▶ Repeat using the picture cards 2–5.

Extension

▶ Continue the activity using picture cards 6–10.

● ● ●

Double 3 is | 6 |

③ Double it!

Learning objective	To consolidate the doubling of numbers to five.
Resources	• picture cards for 3, 4, 5, 6, 8, 10 • number cards 3, 4, 5, 6, 8, 10 • word cards 'three', 'four', 'five', 'six', 'eight', 'ten'
Preparation	Arrange the picture cards randomly over the board.

▶ The aim of the game is to find three pairs, each made of a number and its double, e.g. picture cards for 3 and 6.

▶ Allow the children to volunteer to find the pairs. As each pair is found allow additional volunteers to place the appropriate number cards together at the bottom of the board.

▶ Shuffle the position of the picture cards and repeat.

Extension

▶ Play the same game with only the number cards on the board. Able readers can play the game again using the number word cards.

④ Find half

Learning objective	To introduce halves within the context of number.
Resources	• picture cards for 2, 4, 6, 8, 10 • marker dots of assorted colours • four coloured squares

▶ Place the four squares on the board as follows:

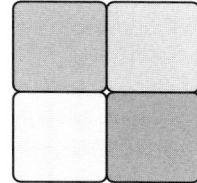

▶ Talk to the children about their understandings of the word 'half'.

▶ Look at the four squares on the board. Pretend that they are pieces of chocolate.

What do we mean by cutting something in half?
If I gave you one of these pieces would that be half of the chocolate?

▶ Emphasise that the two 'halves' of something must be the same size.

How many pieces would be half of the chocolate?
Half of four is two.

▶ Look at each of the picture cards in turn. In each case ask the children to count the objects and then to try to think how many half of them would be.

▶ Use the marker dots to help. For example: represent the six objects on the six buns picture card with six marker dots. Moving the dots around will help children to divide them into two equal sets, discovering that half of 6 is 3.

Extension

▶ Introduce the cards with 12 and 14 objects. How many would half of these numbers be?

⑤ Double it – halve it!

Learning objective	To consolidate knowledge of halves and doubles in working with numbers to 10.
Resources	• number cards 1, 2, 2, 3, 4, 5, 6, 8, 10 • dice labelled 1, 1, 2, 3, 4, 5 • dice labelled 2, 2, 4, 6, 8, 10
Preparation	Arrange the number cards in a grid drawn on the board as shown.

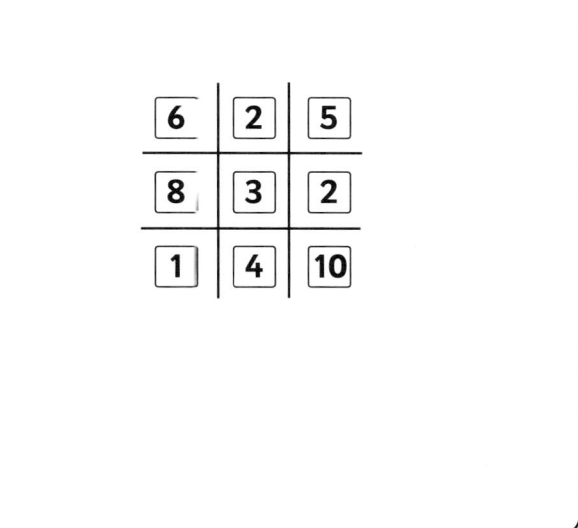

▶ Divide the children into two teams. One team is going to take turns in throwing the dice labelled 2, 2, 4, 6, 8, 10. This team is the 'halving' team.

▶ The other team is going to take turns in throwing the dice labelled 1, 1, 2, 3, 4, 5. This team is the 'doubling' team.

▶ The 'halving' team throws the dice and halves the number thrown (with as much help as necessary). The resulting number is removed from the grid on the board.

▶ Then the 'doubling' team throws their dice and doubles the number thrown. The resulting number is again removed from the grid on the board.

▶ The game is completed when three numbers in a row are removed – horizontally, vertically or diagonally.

▶ When a row of three is completed by removing a number, the team who found that number is the winning team.

▶ The teams exchange roles and the game restarts.

Shape and space

(1) Resources: elephant cards

Place a random selection of elephant cards on the board and encourage children to arrange them in an 'elephant line' according to size.

(2) Resources: elephant cards

Use the elephant cards to make repeating patterns. Use aspects of both colour and size as you create patterns for children to copy and continue.

(3) Resources: elephant cards

Encourage children to build elephant lines using their own patterns. Can the rest of the class identify and continue the pattern?

(4) Resources: coloured squares

Use the coloured squares to build larger rectangular shapes. Sort the shapes built into squares and oblongs.

(5) Resources: 10 x 10 grid overlay, coloured squares, marker dots

Use the 10 x 10 grid to help in building symmetrical patterns. Use one of the vertical or horizontal lines near to the centre of the grid as a line of symmetry. Highlight this line by drawing over it with a marker pen. Arrange a small number of coloured squares or marker dots in the spaces to one side of the line. Can children complete the symmetrical pattern by placing cards in the correction position on the other side of the line?

(6) Resources: elephant cards, monkey cards

Make up a jungle scene using a drawn background and a selection of the animal cards. Use the scene to develop positional language as children follow and give instructions in the placement of cards, or describe the positions of various animals.

(7) Resources: picture cards

Randomly arrange the picture cards in rows on the board. Ask questions: Which picture is above the giraffe? What is between the bees, the rabbits and the parrots? What is below the hedgehogs? Which picture is next to the crabs?

Measure

(1) Resources: elephant cards

Make elephant lines of assorted lengths. Introduce the language of long, longer and longest; short, shorter and shortest.

(2) Resources: elephant cards

Look at the different sized elephant cards.

Which elephant has the shortest trunk?

Which elephant has the longest tail?

Which elephant has the widest ears?

Which elephant would be the heaviest?

Which elephant would be the lightest?

(3) Resources: elephant cards, monkey cards

Use the picture cards as non-standard measures.

How many monkeys make a line about as long as a ruler?

(4) Resources: face cards, coloured squares, marker dots

Use the different-sized cards to encourage children to use appropriate non-standard measures. When measuring a larger item should they use the face cards, coloured squares or marker dots? Which would be better for measuring the length of a small object?

(5) Resources: coloured squares, elephant cards

Use the cards as an activity in becoming familiar with units of time.

How many towers of five squares can you build in a minute?

How many elephant 'families' (large, middle-sized and small) can you put together in half a minute?

(6) Resources: elephant cards, monkey cards

Draw a clock face on the board. Cover some of the numbers with the cards.

Which number is under the blue elephant? Which number is under the monkey?

Which animal would the big hand be pointing to at six o'clock?

Handling data

① **Resources: elephant cards**

Sort the elephants by size and colour.

② **Resources: picture cards**

Use the picture cards as a focus for discussion. Would the children say that any of the cards 'go together'? Encourage children to talk about their ideas.

Use Venn diagrams to record:
– sets and 'not sets', e.g. animals/not animals, food/not food
– discrete sets, e.g. animals/food
– intersecting sets, e.g. animals which fly/animals found in the garden.

③ **Resources: picture cards**

Make a Carrol diagram to sort, for example, animals with or without legs/animals found or not found in the jungle.

④ **Resources: face cards**

Make a Carrol diagram using the ten face cards: girl/not girl, dark hair/not dark hair.

⑤ **Resources: picture cards, coloured squares**

Show the children how to make a simple bar chart by recording the number of objects on each of a selection of picture cards using the coloured squares to make bars.

⑥ **Resources: face cards, coloured squares**

Give a face card to each of ten children in the class. Draw the axes for a simple bar chart on the board. Allow the class to help you to choose an area to investigate, such as favourite crisp flavours, and write the possible categories on the chart. The chart is then compiled as each of the ten children places their card in the appropriate position, recording their chosen response.